Violent Video Game Effects
on Children and Adolescents

VIOLENT VIDEO GAME EFFECTS ON CHILDREN AND ADOLESCENTS

Theory, Research, and Public Policy

Craig A. Anderson
Douglas A. Gentile
Katherine E. Buckley

2007

OXFORD
UNIVERSITY PRESS

Oxford University Press, Inc., publishes works that further
Oxford University's objective of excellence
in research, scholarship, and education.

Oxford   New York
Auckland   Cape Town   Dar es Salaam   Hong Kong   Karachi
Kuala Lumpur   Madrid   Melbourne   Mexico City   Nairobi
New Delhi   Shanghai   Taipei   Toronto

With offices in
Argentina   Austria   Brazil   Chile   Czech Republic   France   Greece
Guatemala   Hungary   Italy   Japan   Poland   Portugal   Singapore
South Korea   Switzerland   Thailand   Turkey   Ukraine   Vietnam

Published by Oxford University Press, Inc.
198 Madison Avenue, New York, New York 10016

www.oup.com

Oxford is a registered trademark of Oxford University Press

Library of Congress Cataloging-in-Publication Data
Anderson, Craig Alan, 1952–
Violent video game effects on children and adolescents : theory, research,
and public policy / by Craig A. Anderson, Douglas A. Gentile, and Katherine E. Buckley.
     p. cm.
Includes bibliographical references and index.
ISBN-13 978-0-19-530983-6
ISBN 0-19-530983-9
1. Video games and children. 2. Video games and teenagers. 3. Violence in mass media.
4. Children and violence. 5. Youth and violence. 6. Aggressiveness in children.
7. Aggressiveness in adolescence.
I. Gentile, Douglas A., 1964–   II. Buckley, Katherine E. III. Title.
HQ784.V53A53 2007
302.23'1—dc22   2006016746

9 8 7 6 5 4

Printed in the United States of America
on acid-free paper

Acknowledgments

This work was supported in part by grants from the Centers for Disease Control and Prevention (CDC), the National Institute of Child Health and Human Development (NICHD), and the Laura Jane Musser Foundation (LJMF). Its contents are solely the responsibility of the authors and do not necessarily represent the official views of the CDC, the NICHD, or the LJMF.

This work benefited greatly from 10 anonymous peer reviews. We gratefully thank these individuals for their wonderful suggestions and comments. In addition, we thank Jennifer Rappaport, the editorial board at Oxford University Press, and countless colleagues and students who contributed in one way or another to this work.

Contents

Part III. General Discussion (What Does It All Mean?)

PART I

INTRODUCTION

In Part I we describe the basic issues concerning violent video games, past research, and our theoretical approach. Chapter 1 presents a brief history of violent video games, youth exposure to such games, and an overview of things to come. Chapter 2 lays out a host of conceptual viewpoints involving definitions, methodologies, and guiding principles. It then provides a brief review of prior media violence research, with a special emphasis on research involving the effects of violent video games. Chapter 3 presents the General Aggression Model in somewhat more detail, and shows how that model can be used to understand developmental processes and a risk and resilience approach to human aggression. It concludes with a section on how the General Aggression Model can be used to understand and predict effects of media violence on the development of aggressive behavior and aggressive personality.

1

Violent Video Games: Background and Overview

Violent video games are popular with male and female children, adolescents, and adults. They have been successfully marketed to youth and are easily obtained regardless of age (e.g., Buchman & Funk, 1996; Federal Trade Commission, 2000; Walsh, 1999). Even the U.S. government has created and distributes violent video games to youths, and does so without checking the ages of those to whom it distributes the game (i.e., the game *America's Army*, which can be downloaded from the Internet or can be obtained from recruiting offices).

Public attention and debate about violent video games has been one of the few positive outcomes of the horrendous spate of school shootings by boys with a history of playing violent video games [e.g., West Paducah, Kentucky (December, 1997); Jonesboro, Arkansas (March, 1998); Springfield, Oregon (May, 1998), Littleton, Colorado (April, 1999), Santee, California (March, 2001), Wellsboro, Pennsylvania (June, 2003) and Red Lion, Pennsylvania (April, 2003)]. Other violent crimes have also been linked by the news media to violent video games, including a violent crime spree in Oakland, California (January, 2003); five homicides in Long Prairie and Minneapolis, Minnesota (May, 2003); beating deaths in Medina, Ohio (November, 2002) and Wyoming, Michigan (November, 2002); and the Washington, DC, "Beltway" sniper shootings (Fall, 2002). As early as 2000 the U.S. Federal Bureau of Investigation included "fascination with violence-filled entertainment" as one of the warning signs characteristic of school shooters (O'Toole, 2000, p. 20). More directly relevant to video games, this report noted that the high-risk student "spends inordinate amounts of time playing video games with violent

3

themes, and seems more interested in the violent images than in the game itself. On the Internet, the student regularly searches for Web sites involving violence, weapons, and other disturbing subjects" (O'Toole, 2000, p. 20).

Frequent associations with violent crimes do not, in themselves, constitute strong scientific evidence that exposure to violent video games is a contributing causal factor in violent behavior. Nevertheless, the scientific debate about whether exposure to media violence causes increases in aggressive behavior is over (Anderson, Berkowitz, Donnerstein, Huesmann, Johnson, Linz, Malamuth, and Wartella, 2003; Gentile, 2003; Kirsh, 2006; Potter, 2003) and should have been over 30 years ago (Bushman & Anderson, 2001). The entire body of relevant media violence research stretches back over 50 years and includes studies on violent television, films, video games, music, and even comic books. Populations studied include males and females; young children, adolescents, and adults; criminals and noncriminals; highly aggressive and nonaggressive people. All major types of research methodologies have been used, including experiments, cross-sectional correlational studies, longitudinal studies, intervention studies, and meta-analyses. Anderson and Bushman (2002b) summarized much of this work and included meta-analytic results on four categories of media violence work: laboratory experiments, field experiments, cross-sectional correlational studies, and longitudinal studies. For each category exposure to media violence was significantly associated with increased aggression or violence.

A panel of leading media violence researchers organized by Professor Rowell Huesmann (originally at the request of the U.S. Surgeon General) conducted the most comprehensive review to date of media violence effects on aggression and aggression-related variables. This panel found "unequivocal evidence that media violence increases the likelihood of aggressive and violent behavior in both immediate and long-term contexts" (Anderson et al., 2003, p. 81). This report also found that the effects tend to be smaller for more severe forms of violence than for milder forms. Nonetheless, the range of effect sizes on severe forms of violence are substantial even when compared to other violence risk factors (e.g., abusive parents) or to a variety of medical risk factors seen as significant enough to warrant action by the medical and public health communities (e.g., asbestos exposure and laryngeal cancer). Furthermore, there have been significant advances in theoretical accounts of human aggression in general, accounts that also incorporate media violence effects (e.g., Anderson et al., 2003; Anderson & Bushman, 2002a; Anderson & Huesmann, 2003).

Nonetheless, there are numerous unanswered questions in need of additional research. For example, the video game research literature is much smaller than the combined TV and film literature, and there are gaps in the video game literature. As of this writing, there are no published longitudinal studies that isolate violent video game effects on aggression, though a couple of studies link overall video game playing time to aggressive behavior longitudinally (Ihori, Sakamoto, Kobayashi, & Kimura, 2003; Slater, Henry, Swaim, & Anderson, 2003). Another question in need of additional research concerns whether media violence causes greater increases in aggression for children than for adolescents and young adults. There is some correlational and longitudinal evidence supporting such a youth vulnerability hypothesis, and there are good theoretical reasons to expect such an effect, but there also is evidence that even young adults can be adversely affected by repeated exposure to media violence. The new studies reported in this monograph address a number of such unresolved issues with a focus on violent video game effects. Before further exploring the theoretical issues in greater detail, we examine data on the characteristics and usage of video games.

A Brief History

Video games first emerged in the 1970s, but it was during the 1990s that violent games truly came of age. Starting in the late 1980s video game producers experimented with what the public would accept in video games. Gradually it became clear that games sold better if they contained more violence. One-on-one fighting games such as *Double Dragon* and *Mortal Kombat* pushed the boundaries of violence and became all-time best sellers. Nintendo (the clear market leader in the late 1980s and early 1990s), like Atari before them, had game standards, including "No excessive blood and violence" and "No sex" (Kent, 2001, p. 465). But the economic benefits of increased violence and gore became apparent when both Nintendo and Sega created versions of Mortal Kombat for their competing systems. Nintendo had toned down the blood and gore in their version, and the Sega Genesis version outsold Nintendo's version three to one, leading to Nintendo's decline as the market leader and to the conclusion that violence sells video games to children.

At this point in time the violence in video games was still fairly stylized, in large part because of technological constraints, although it was becoming more realistic. In 1992, *Wolfenstein 3D*, the first major "first-person shooter" game was released. In a first-person shooter, one "sees" the video game world through the eyes of the player, rather than seeing it as if looking on from afar (as in almost all of the previous fighting games). The player can move around, exploring a three-dimensional environment and shooting at various game characters. The effect is to make the game player feel as though he or she is in the game and is the one fighting, killing, and being killed. This additional realism was followed by other realistic touches. Video game historian Steven Kent noted that "part of *Wolfenstein*'s popularity sprang from its shock value. In previous games, when players shot enemies, the injured targets fell and disappeared. In *Wolfenstein 3D*, enemies fell and bled on the floor" (Kent, 2001, p. 458). This caused a revolution in the way violent games were designed. By 1993 the next major first-person shooter, *Doom*, included more blood and gore. It also allowed players to hunt and kill each other as well as monsters and demons.

The advances in technology over the past few years have been remarkable. Electronic game images are composed of polygons, making polygons per second a good measure of graphic quality. The original Sony *PlayStation* processed 350,000 polygons per second (pg/s). Sega *Dreamcast*, released in 1999, boosted that to over 3 million, and *PlayStation 2* rocketed to 66 million pg/s. Microsoft's *Xbox*, released in 2001, increased graphic capability to 125 million pg/s. The stated goal for *PlayStation 3* is 1 billion pg/s. The dramatic increase in speed and graphic capability has allowed for more realistic violence than ever before possible. For example, in 2000 the game *Soldier of Fortune* (SOF) was released for personal computers, marking a new high in video game violence realism. This first-person shooter game was designed in collaboration with an ex-army colonel, and features 26 different "killing zones" in the body. The characters in the game respond realistically to different shots depending on where in the body they are shot, with what weapons, and from what distance. For example, shooting a character in the arm at close range with a shotgun rips the arm from the socket, leaving exposed bone and sinew while blood rushes from the wound. Of course now, in this first decade of the twenty-first century, even more graphically violent games are available to virtually anyone who wants to play them, regardless of age, and there is evidence that children are spending increasing amounts of time playing video games.

Youth Exposure

In the mid-1980s, children averaged about 4 hours a week playing video games, including time spent playing at home and in arcades (Harris & Williams, 1985). By the early 1990s, home video game use had increased and arcade play had decreased. The average amount was still fairly low, averaging about 2 hours of home play per week for girls, and about 4 hours of home play per week for boys (Funk, 1993). By the mid 1990s, home use had increased for fourth-grade girls to 4.5 hours per week, and to 7.1 hours per week for fourth-grade boys (Buchman & Funk, 1996). This same sample of fourth-graders reported that most of their favorite games were violent (59% for girls, 73% for boys). According to recent national surveys of parents, school-age children (boys and girls combined) devote about 7 hours per week playing video games (Gentile & Walsh, 2002; Woodard & Gridina, 2000). In a recent survey of over 600 eighth- and ninth-grade students, children averaged 9 hours per week of video game play overall, with boys averaging 13 hours per week and girls averaging 5 hours per week (Gentile, Lynch, Linder, & Walsh, 2004). In the present research (Study 3), it appears that the amount may still be increasing. Thus, although sex-correlated differences in the amount of time committed to playing video games continue to exist, both boys and girls are spending more time with video games. Somewhat surprising, the amount of time children devote to television has remained remarkably stable even as the amount of time devoted to video and computer games has increased.

Data from the Cooperative Institutional Research Program (CIRP, 1998, 2005), which surveys entering college freshmen from over 600 two- and four-year colleges, reveal that older students also are playing a lot of video games, and that their time with such games is also increasing. In 1998 13.3% of the young men reported playing video games at least 6 hours per week during their senior year in high school. By 2005 that figure had increased to 21.4%. Increases are also occurring at the high end of the game playing distribution. In 1998, 2% of the young men reported playing video games over 20 hours per week; by 2005, that figure had increased to 3.2%.

The prevalence of video games in the lives of youth is not only an American phenomenon. For example, a recent national study of 3,442 6- to 65-year-olds in the United Kingdom revealed that children are the most likely group to play video games, with 100% of 6- to 10-year-olds, 97% of 11- to 15-year-olds, and 82% of 16- to 24-year-olds playing video games at least occasionally (Pratchett, 2005).

A related aspect to children's involvement in video games concerns the lack of parental or societal oversight. Among eighth- and ninth-grade students, only 15% said their parents "always" or "often" check the video game ratings before allowing them to buy or rent video games; over half (53%) said they "never" do (Gentile et al., 2004). Furthermore, only one in five parents have ever kept their children from getting a game because of its rating (Gentile et al., 2004; Walsh, Gentile, Gieske, Walsh, & Chasco, 2003). Further complicating matters is the finding that ratings provided by the video game industry do not match those provided by other adults and game-playing youngsters. Specifically, many games involving violence by cartoon-like characters are classified by the industry as being appropriate for general audiences, a classification with which adults and youngsters disagree (Funk, Flores, Buchman, & Germann, 1999). The only ratings category for which parents and industry ratings unanimously agree is the "mature" category; almost half (43%) of parents disagree with the "teen" category ratings (Walsh & Gentile, 2001). Content analyses of teen-rated games show that in almost half of the cases (48%), the games include potentially objectionable content that the official content descriptors for the game do not describe (Haninger & Thompson, 2004). Thus, even if parents more frequently used the provided ratings, many children would still be exposed to content their parents did not intend them to see (for a review of issues regarding media ratings in general, see Gentile, Humphrey, & Walsh, 2005).

Parents also are not heavily involved in the amount of time children play video games. Eighty-nine percent of the teens in Walsh's (2000) survey reported that their parents never put limits on how much time they are allowed to play video games. Furthermore, many violent games have "demo" versions on the Internet that can be downloaded for free by anyone. Of the boys in Walsh's (2000) sample who play video games, 32% reported downloading them from the Internet. Similarly, Larson has argued that "parents' ability to regulate media use seems to be declining" (2001, p. 150). In recent years, as high-speed Internet access has increased, so has the availability of free Internet-based violent video games, sometimes developed by hate groups targeting specific victims or types of victims.

Theoretical Overview and Things to Come

Developmental scientists have been concerned about the effects of screen-based media violence on children for decades (c.f., Siegel, 1958). This concern has led to a phenomenal amount of high-quality research on the many effects, the many mechanisms, and the many potential moderators and mediators of the effects. As the data have accumulated, theories have also undergone a great deal of development. Several theories that tie media to child development have been supported by research evidence. These theories have been developed to predict and explain both short-term and long-term effects (e.g., general arousal theory, excitation transfer theory, social learning theory/social cognitive theory, cognitive neoassociation theory, script theory, cultivation theory, desensitization theory, displacement theory). Some of the theories were specifically developed to account for media violence effects (e.g., cultivation theory). Others focus on a particular psychological process, such as excitation transfer theory's focus on arousal. In general, each of the theories that have a long-term aspect is an attempt to describe the same developmental story. Specifically, children who consume violent media incorporate aggressive concepts and behaviors into their typical behavioral repertoire, and thus become more aggressive over time. What differs among these theories is the proposed mechanisms mediating the processes by which these developmental changes occur.

It is both one of the strengths and one of the weaknesses of theory in this area that these theories are not mutually exclusive. It is very difficult to design studies that could provide critical tests between them, although it has been done in some rare cases (D. Anderson, Huston, Schmitt, Linebarger, & Wright, 2001). In fact, it is likely that these theories are *all* correct under the right circumstances.

The pattern of theoretical development in the media violence domain is similar to other trends in developmental psychological theories (e.g., for a review and synthesis in antisocial development, see Dodge & Petit, 2003). In the middle of the last century, theories tended to be general theories, usually focused on learning. In the 1970s, focus shifted to more detailed theories of specific phenomena and processes. By the 1990s, this had resulted in many excellent theories, but they were "a loose array of diverse predictors of antisocial development, without integration or an understanding of how these predictors operate together" (Dodge & Petit, 2003). In response to this concern, more recent theories have begun to incorporate several of these specific theories into broader, more general theories. Some of them focus on cognitive aspects, such as Huesmann's social-cognitive theory (e.g., Huesmann, Moise-Titus, Podolski, & Eron, 2003). Social-cognitive theory postulates long-term effects of media violence exposure on aggression by observational learning that affects one or more of three social-cognitive structures: hostile world schemas (e.g., hostile attribution bias), social problem-solving scripts, and normative beliefs about the acceptability of aggression. Other recent theoretical developments include attempting to model as many of the above processes as possible with one overarching framework, such as Anderson and colleagues' General Aggression Model (Anderson & Bushman, 2002a; Anderson & Carnagey, 2004; Anderson & Huesmann, 2003), which will be described in more detail in a later section.

One interesting feature of most extant theories of media violence effects is that they are seldom considered to be true developmental theories (Kirsh, 2003). For example, script theory and cognitive neo-association theory are basically learning theories, but not developmental. In our estimation, this is an important observation because it demands a consideration of what makes a theory "developmental." Much developmental research uses age as a proxy for developmental variables. Age, by itself, is not an independent variable. Age does not cause any effects, nor does it explain any. Positing age differences alone does not make a theory developmental, in our view.

So, what is correlated with age that might account for observed age differences and might be seen as truly developmental? One example might be different cognitive abilities that tend to occur at certain ages (e.g., concrete operational thinking at age 8 compared to formal operational thinking at age 16). Yet it is our opinion that merely positing that different abilities might moderate the effect of media violence still does not make a theory developmental.

What truly makes a theory developmental—in our view—is its ability to understand and predict *change* across time in addition to predicting how age-correlated abilities might moderate the effects (or might not). In this sense, learning theories are developmental theories. Over the past 20 years, there have been several theoretical advances made in developmental theories to predict individual differences, both in normal and atypical development. One of these advances has been the development of risk and resilience models, similar to those used in public health. Risk and resilience models begin from the empirical finding that several variables are usually comorbid (Pettit, 2004). For example, a violent child usually has many problems in his or her life, each of which is predictive of aggressive behavior (risk factors), and few supportive variables that are predictive of healthy outcomes (protective factors). To be considered a truly developmental risk factor for aggressive behavior, a variable must have both a theoretical rationale and an empirically demonstrated ability to predict aggressive behavior (e.g., U.S. Department of Health and Human Services, 2001). "How risk and protective factors . . . coalesce and interact with one another to increase (or decrease) the probability of violent behavior has been a central theme in recent research on the developmental course of antisocial behavior" (Petit, 2004). A strength of this approach is its ability to predict developmental trajectories across childhood and adolescence (Petit & Dodge, 2003).

In this monograph, we focus on the General Aggression Model (GAM) as a basis for explaining and predicting the short-term effects of violent video games, long-term effects of violent video games, and *changes* in aggression related to exposure to violent video games. We also describe how two approaches based on theories of developmental psychopathology can be integrated with the General Aggression Model to enhance our understanding of how we can predict long-term changes based on violent media exposure in conjunction with other risk factors for aggression, as well as how we can predict how children of different ages might show differential effects of media exposure. But first, we elucidate key points concerning various research methods for studying the effects of violent video games, and review previous research on violent video game effects. We then give a detailed description of the General Aggression Model and its ability to handle developmental issues and to integrate a wide array of findings both within and outside of the media violence domain. In later sections we present three new studies of violent video games. We conclude with a general discussion of several key issues, including developmental issues, the failure of catharsis theory, and public policy.

2

Effects of Exposure to Violent Entertainment Media

There are hundreds of articles and chapters in edited volumes on violent television and film effects, and dozens on the topic of violent video game effects. Among the earliest video game studies was a correlational study of time spent playing arcade video games and self-reported aggression and delinquency by Dominick (1984). There have been numerous narrative reviews of the media violence effects studies (for television and film, e.g., Bushman & Huesmann, 2001; Comstock, 1980; Geen & Thomas, 1986; Huesmann & Miller, 1994; Huesmann, Moise, & Podolski, 1997; Smith & Donnerstein, 1998; Strasburger & Wilson, 2003; for video games, e.g., Dill & Dill, 1998). Similarly, there have been a number of meta-analytic reviews of this research (for television and film, e.g., Comstock & Scharrer, 2003; Hearold, 1986; Paik & Comstock, 1994; Wood, Wong, & Cachere, 1991; for video games, e.g., Anderson, 2004; Anderson & Bushman, 2001; Sherry, 2001). Every major review has found significant effects of media violence on aggression. Before summarizing the results of prior research in more detail, it is important to consider a few definitional and methodological issues.

Definitions of Aggression

Scholars and others writing about human aggression and violence sometimes use the same term to describe conceptually different ideas. For example, "aggression" has sometimes referred to measures as varied as behaviors that harmed another person, intentions to harm someone, and thoughts or feelings about harming oneself or others. This has led to some confusion and a somewhat artificial debate on how many studies of "aggression" are in the research literature. Social psychologists and most human aggression researchers have adopted a much more precise definition, one that will be used throughout this monograph. Human aggression is defined as (a) a behavior that is intended to harm another individual, (b) the behavior is expected by the perpetrator to have some chance of actually harming that individual, and (c) the perpetrator believes that the target individual is motivated to avoid the harm. Under this definition, accidental harm is not aggressive because it is not intentional. Harm necessitated by service to a higher goal (e.g., pain caused by a dental procedure) is not aggressive because the target individual (patient) seeks out the higher goal. (See Anderson & Huesmann, 2003; Baron & Richardson, 1994; Berkowitz, 1993; Bushman & Anderson, 2001; and Geen, 2001, for more detailed discussions.)

Subtypes of Aggression

Aggression has been further divided into subtypes in several different ways, such as direct versus indirect, and affective (or hostile) versus instrumental. Though these distinctions have been important in some contexts, they sometimes create additional problems (Anderson & Huesmann, 2003; Bushman & Anderson, 2001). We focus on four subtypes in this monograph, but recognize that in other contexts some other distinctions may also be useful.

Physical Aggression and Violence

The first subtype, *physical aggression*, involves causing harm by direct physical means, such as by hitting, tripping, stabbing, or shooting. *Violence* is simply one form of physical aggression, at the high end of a severity dimension. In the past, some human aggression scholars treated violence and aggression as though they were totally different concepts. Indeed, some scholarly fields still tend to do so, in part because of legal definitions. For example, *violence* is sometimes reserved for aggressive acts that are also criminal. However, in recent years there has been a convergence of opinion among *psychological* scholars that physical aggression should be conceived as existing along a severity continuum ranging from mild (e.g., a pinch) to severe (e.g., shooting), and that violence (or violent behavior) refers to physical aggression toward the severe end of this continuum (e.g., Anderson et al., 2003; Anderson & Huesmann, 2003).

Verbal Aggression

A second type, *verbal aggression*, involves causing harm by verbal means, such as by calling a person hurtful names. Verbal aggression also includes written statements (including e-mail, Web pages) that attempt to cause harm or evaluations of others (verbal or written) that are intended to harm the target person.

Relational Aggression

A third type, called *relational aggression*, consists of behaviors that harm others through damage (or the threat of damage) to relationships or to feelings of acceptance, friendship, or group inclusion (Crick, 1996; see Crick et al., 1999, for a review). Children who spread rumors, exclude peers, and engage in other relationship-oriented aggression often are different from those who hit or kick to harm another person.

Physical and relational forms of aggression are moderately correlated, which is to be expected, given that they are both forms of aggressive behavior (Crick et al., 1999). Nonetheless, relational aggression emerges as a distinct form of aggression and studies have begun to focus on the possible differential correlates of these subtypes (Crick, 1995; Crick et al., 1999). To our knowledge, no study has yet compared physically and relationally aggressive children in terms of their violent media consumption habits (except for one study of preschoolers, who do not consume much media violence; Ostrov, Gentile, & Crick, in press). Substantial evidence suggests that females are more likely to engage in relational aggression, males are more likely to engage in physical aggression and violence, and both sexes are about equally likely to engage in verbal aggression (Anderson & Huesmann, 2003; Bjorkqvist, Lagerspetz, & Kaukiainen, 1992; Crick & Grotpeter, 1995; Lagerspetz, Bjorkqvist, & Peltonen, 1988; Lagerspetz & Bjorkqvist, 1992).

Research and Review Methodologies

In this section we briefly describe the main research and review methods used by modern sciences. For many readers of this monograph, this section will be a review that can be skipped. For others, this section is intended to set the stage for subsequent sections describing prior video game research, our three new studies, and our conclusions from those studies.

Experimental, Cross-Section Correlational, and Longitudinal Studies

Three Types of Studies

Generally, one can divide original empirical research studies into one of three categories based on research method—experimental, cross-section correlational, or longitudinal. Each has its own pattern of strengths and weaknesses. Experimental studies are those in which the researcher randomly assigns participants to different treatment and control conditions. For example, participants might be randomly assigned to play either a violent or a nonviolent video game prior to measuring aggressive responses to a provocation. The main strength of experimental studies is that they allow the strongest causal inferences. This is because random assignment dramatically reduces the possibility that the comparison groups differed at the outset in ways that could yield statistically significant differences in the key outcome (or dependent) measure. In other words, random assignment allows the researcher to rule out a host of alternative explanations of the obtained differences between the violent and nonviolent video game conditions. If the treatment and control conditions yield different results on the aggression measure, then it is very likely that the experimental manipulation (e.g., video game type) caused the difference, and very unlikely that the naturally most aggressive individuals happened to wind up in the violent video game condition. The main weakness of experimental studies is that for ethical reasons one cannot measure the most serious levels of aggression. For example, one cannot randomly assign newborn babies to grow up in either a high versus low media violence environment, and then follow them for 40 years or so to see which group ends up committing the most violent crimes.

Cross-section correlational studies (usually simply called *correlational* studies) are those in which the independent variables (e.g., level of habitual exposure to violent video games) and dependent variables (e.g., frequency of fighting at school) are measured once, more or less at the same point in time. For example, a researcher might ask adolescents to fill out questionnaires that assess their media use habits, aggressive tendencies, and some personality variables. The main strength of such correlational studies is that even extreme types of aggression can be measured, such as using force to get money from other people (i.e., robbery, assault). The main weakness of correlational studies is that causality is much more difficult to establish. For example, if the only variables assessed in a particular correlational study are amount of weekly violent video game play and number of fights at school in the past year, even a strong positive correlation does not guarantee that video game violence exposure causally contributed to the fighting behavior. It is possible that children who are naturally more aggressive (for whatever biological, cultural, familial, or environmental reasons) also happen to prefer more violent video games. In other words, there remains a plausible alternative explanation of the finding that high video game violence exposure was statistically associated with high aggression, an alternative that does not require assigning a causal role to video game violence exposure.

Longitudinal studies are those in which the independent and dependent variables are assessed at two or more points in time, separated by theoretically meaningful time intervals. For example, a researcher might assess aggressive behavioral tendencies and media habits for the same group of 10-year-old children at the beginning and end of a school year. The main advantages of longitudinal designs are two-fold: (a) consequential, real-world aggression can be assessed (e.g., fighting at school); (b) it is easier to establish causality because one can rule out a host of key alternative explanations. Specifically, if media violence exposure measured at the beginning of the school year predicts aggression levels at the end of the school year even after statistically controlling for aggressive behavioral tendencies that existed at the beginning of the school year, then one key alternative explanation of media violence–aggression correlations—that aggressive children simply like aggressive entertainment media—is essentially disconfirmed.

Other Considerations

Of course, in the research world there are many more considerations than those mentioned here. Within each of these three study types, some studies are better conducted than others. The better studies attempt to control for theoretically relevant variables, use the most appropriate measures of key conceptual variables, use appropriate sample sizes, and avoid the numerous pitfalls associated with that particular domain of study. Poorer ones fail to do so.

For example, correlational studies of the link between video game violence exposure and aggression need minimally to have a good measure of amount of exposure to violent video games (not just a measure of total video game time) and a good measure of aggression (typically, not a single self-rated aggressive behavior item). In addition, the researcher should be aware of broader historical and socioeconomic factors that may distort the findings, and know the likely direction of that distortion. For instance, we know that video games didn't become very violent until the early 1990s. We also know that in the United States, socioeconomic status is negatively associated with aggression levels of children, youth, and adults. Youth from poorer backgrounds tend to behave more aggressively for a wide array of reasons. We also know that access to computer and video games in the home was positively associated with socioeconomic status, especially in the early years of the computer revolution (i.e., the 1980s and early 1990s). Wealthier families were more likely to have some type of video game playing system (e.g., computers, video game consoles) than poorer families. These latter two facts thus created a research situation (during the 1980s and early 1990s, possibly later) with a built-in bias; children who were most likely to be aggressive (for socioeconomic and related reasons) were also least likely to have much access to video games at all, either violent or nonviolent. This built-in bias worked against the media violence hypothesis, because it artifactually creates a negative relation between video game violence exposure and aggression in correlational studies. If such correlational studies yield the predicted positive correlation, it is in spite of this built-in bias, not because of it. In sum, one of the worst possible ways to test the violent video game hypothesis in a correlational design would be to (a) rely on data gathered before the mid-1990s, (b) use a poor measure of aggression, (c) use a measure of computer game play rather than violent video game play, (d) ignore potential socioeconomic confounds. Such a test is heavily biased against the hypothesis that exposure to violent video games causes an increase in aggression. If such a study found a nonsignificant correlation or even a significant negative correlation between amount of video game play and aggression, it would mean almost nothing. Unfortunately, such poor studies have been conducted, published, and misinterpreted (e.g., Durkin & Barber, 2002).

Another example of poor methodology getting in the way of generally useful methods concerns dropout rates. This is important in all types of studies but is particularly problematic in experimental studies. As noted earlier, the primary strength of experimental studies derives from the fact that participants are *randomly* assigned to the different conditions of an experiment (e.g., half to play a violent video game, the other half to play a nonviolent video game), therefore making it likely that the groups will be fairly equivalent on relevant unmeasured dimensions. For example, both groups will contain similar proportions of naturally aggressive and nonaggressive individuals. Thus, observed differences between the randomly assigned conditions that emerge after the experimental treatment has been applied are likely to be the result of the different treatments, not preexisting differences between the groups. However, if a significant portion of participants drop out of the study after random assignment has taken place, then the study loses the key feature of a true experiment and becomes impossible to interpret. One recent example of such a study is Williams and

Skoric (2005), which will be further discussed in a later section on longitudinal video game studies.

Mixed Designs

Many of the best studies combine several design features. Most recent experimental studies of violent video games also include correlational aspects. For example, Uhlmann and Swanson (2004) randomly assigned participants to play either a violent or nonviolent video game prior to completing an implicit measure of aggressive self-concept. (This measures the extent to which a person views himself or herself as an aggressive person, and does so in a way that is not at all obvious to the person whose self-concept is being measured.) Prior habitual exposure to violent video games was also assessed as an individual difference measure. Participant sex (male versus female) was another individual difference variable included in the study. Results showed that the experimental manipulation of exposure to video game violence caused a significant shift in implicit self-concept; playing the violent game yielded a more aggressive self-concept than playing the nonviolent game. This occurred for both males and females. In addition, habitual exposure to violent video games was positively associated with aggressive self-concept. Finally, statistically controlling for habitual exposure to violent video games led to a slightly larger effect of the experimental manipulation of video game violence on implicit aggressive self-concept.

The inclusion of appropriate individual difference variables in experimental designs is advantageous for several reasons. First, inclusion of such variables allows additional tests of key hypotheses. Uhlmann and Swanson (2004), for instance, were able to test for both short-term experimental and longer-term correlational effects of video game violence exposure on implicit aggressive self-concept. Second, including individual difference variables can often reduce the error term in the statistical analyses, which increases the likelihood that the study will be able to detect true experimental effects. Third, including individual difference variables allows tests of whether particular subgroups are relatively more or less susceptible to the experimental manipulation. Uhlmann and Swanson, for instance, demonstrated that both males and females were influenced by the brief exposure to the violent video game.

Of course, sometimes experimental manipulations are so powerful that they temporarily overwhelm individual difference effects (e.g., Anderson, 1983). In such cases, one must be careful to not overinterpret the lack of a significant individual difference effect.

Narrative and Meta-Analytic Reviews

The traditional literature review, in which all relevant published empirical studies are described, categorized, and summarized, is known as the *narrative* review. For example, one might review the research studies on the effects of smoking on lung cancer. The major strength of narrative reviews is the focus on conceptual similarities and differences among the different empirical studies being reviewed. This focus often leads to rich theoretical and methodological insights, which in turn can lead to new hypotheses and revised theoretical models. But different studies necessarily yield somewhat different results. Even if a study is repeated with exactly the same methods the results are very likely to differ to some extent. (Imagine tossing a coin 10 times, recording the percentage of "heads" to see whether it is a "fair" coin, then repeating this process.) How does one make sense of these differing results? What does one conclude about the overall (or average) effect of the independent variable (smoking) on the dependent variable (lung cancer)? The major weakness, then, is that many of the critical decisions and distinctions made while attempting to understand the various methodologies and results are subjective. This opens the door for reviewer biases, which can (and sometimes does) result in widely different interpretations of the empirical literature by reviewers with different biases.

Meta-analytic reviews also attempt to include all relevant empirical studies, both published and unpublished. A *meta-analysis* consists of using statistical techniques to combine the results of many empirical studies of a particular hypothesis. For example, Anderson and Bushman (2001) reported the first comprehensive meta-analysis of violent video game studies. They found 33 independent tests (with a total of 3,033 research participants) of the hypothesis that higher exposure to violent video games would be linked to higher levels of aggressive behavior. Using standard meta-analytic techniques, they averaged the effects of these 33 tests and found that on average the hypothesized effect was supported statistically at a level beyond any reasonable doubt. This statistical averaging across all relevant studies results in an objective statistical summary of the research literature, including an overall estimate of the effect size (e.g., how big is the effect of exposure to violent video games on aggressive behavior) and a statistical test of whether the average effect is statistically larger or smaller than zero (i.e., no effect). Thus, one major strength of meta-analytic reviews is their objectivity. Meta-analytic reviews of the same general research question generally yield the same or very similar answers, regardless of the different perspectives from which different reviewers begin (e.g., all major meta-analytic reviews of the media violence studies). The second major strength of meta-analytic reviews is that by consolidating results across multiple studies of the same hypothesis, they can overcome weaknesses and illusory inconsistencies that result from too-small sample sizes. (Imagine tossing a coin twice, recording the percentage of "heads," and repeating this process 100 times. The results of these 100 "studies" of the coin's fairness will seem quite inconsistent, sometimes appearing to favor "heads," sometimes favoring "tails," and sometimes appearing "fair." By combining the results across these 100 studies, one gets a much more accurate view of the true fairness of the coin.)

There still are, of course, difficult decisions faced by the meta-analytic reviewer. For example, in some studies there are several possible comparison groups that could be used; which ones are deemed most appropriate may vary somewhat from one reviewer to another. Nonetheless, the subjectivity problem inherent in narrative reviews is much reduced in the meta-analytic review, as is the problem of small-sample-size-based illusions of inconsistency.

The major weakness of meta-analytic reviews is that sometimes the reviewers get so focused on the statistical aspects that they can easily forget or ignore important conceptual aspects. But a good meta-analytic review can include the conceptual aspects. Indeed, if the research literature is sufficiently large and varied, some key conceptual issues can be addressed meta-analytically (see Paik & Comstock, 1994). For example, the Anderson and Bushman (2001) meta-analytic review of the video game literature tested for differences in effect size for experimental versus correlational studies, older versus younger participants, and published versus unpublished studies, and found no significant differences. These conceptually based comparisons demonstrated that the obtained effects of violent video games were consistent across type of study, age, and publication status, thereby increasing confidence in the validity, generality, and pervasiveness of these effects.

Science, Causality, and Alternative Explanations

Very often, scientists differ on issues of preferred research method, comfort in making causal statements, and willingness to generalize. We cannot claim any special insights regarding these and related philosophy of science issues, but we believe that several rather general principles accurately describe how most modern science (at least, behavioral science) operates.

These principles guide our analysis of past research in this domain as well as our own new research contributions, so we believe the reader should be aware of these principles.

Scientific Theories or Models Are Causal

There are very few instances in which major scientific theories in any domain of science are not based on causal principles. The hallmarks of good theory—prediction and control—require causal models. This does not deny that some theories (and sciences) are based primarily on correlational data; the laws of planetary motion have never been tested by randomly assigning planets to various locations in order to observe their effects on other planets, yet astronomy is a science with causal laws. Similarly, at a given point in time a particular scientific theory may not have generated sufficient evidence to conclude that its causal precepts are without doubt true, but that does not mean that the basic structure of that theory isn't causal.

Scientific Causality Is Often Probabilistic

The old Logic 101 principles regarding the establishment of a factor as being a necessary and sufficient cause of an effect simply don't apply to most modern science (Anderson & Bushman, 2002c). We know that smoking tobacco causes an increase in the likelihood that one will contract lung cancer, but not everyone who smokes gets cancer, and some who don't smoke do get lung cancer. The probabilistic nature of modern science is largely due to the fact that multiple causal factors are involved in most medical, psychological, and behavioral phenomena. And for this reason, the old necessary and sufficient rules simply do not apply. Thus, every time people argue that violent video games can't be considered causes of aggression because they have played such games and haven't killed anyone is committing a major reasoning error, applying the "sufficient" rule to a multiple cause phenomenon. A similarly invalid argument is that the reduction in U.S. homicide rates during the 1990s—while violent video games were becoming more prevalent—proves that violent video games can't cause increases in aggression. This argument assumes either that violence is not caused by multiple factors, or that those factors are unchanging over time. Neither assumption is true (consider, for example, changes in overall incarceration rates, federal gun registration laws, drug use patterns, age distribution of the population, poverty rates, employment patterns, war), rendering the argument so weak as to be embarrassing.

Establishing Causality Largely Involves Ruling Out Plausible Alternative Explanations

Creating and testing scientific theories (which are necessarily causal, in our view) involves creating plausible explanatory networks of ideas, testing those ideas by looking for plausible alternative explanations and gathering relevant data, and then either rejecting the alternative explanations or revising the explanatory network. As the plausibility of reasonable alternative explanations declines, the strength of the remaining (and revised) causal explanatory network (i.e., the scientific theory) grows. It is for this reason that even purely cross-section correlational data are relevant to establishing causality. Such data often provide opportunities for the testing of alternative explanations. When the alternative explanations fail, and the target causal hypothesis holds up, the overarching theoretical explanation gains strength. When the alternative explanations succeed or when the target causal hypothesis does not hold up, the overarching theoretical explanation loses strength, perhaps requiring revision of the theory.

Different Methodologies Allow Triangulation on the Most Plausible Causal Model

The principle of triangulation is widely used both within and outside science. When the same phenomenon is viewed from multiple perspectives and yields the same answer, we should have much more confidence in that answer than when only one perspective is used or when different perspectives yield different answers. Thus, when experimental and correlational and longitudinal studies conducted with various participant populations and methodologies converge on the same answer, we should begin to believe that answer. Or as Richard Cardinal Cushing put it (when asked about the propriety of calling Fidel Castro a communist), "When I see a bird that walks like a duck and swims like a duck and quacks like a duck, I call that bird a duck" (New York Times, 1964). As noted very early in this monograph, the broader media violence research literature has clearly identified its "duck" (Anderson et al., 2003).

Conceptual Relations Between Variables Generalize

In periodic fits of self-castigation, behavioral scientists bemoan the discrepancies between laboratory procedures and measures and events in the real world. There have been several excellent answers to such complaints (e.g., Banaji & Crowder, 1989; Berkowitz & Donnerstein, 1982; Kruglanski, 1975; Mook, 1983). Perhaps the most relevant in this context is that conceptual variables generalize, even if specific operationalizations do not. For example, one of the best predictors of aggression is provocation. As one of us discovered many years ago, for preschoolers at a daycare facility in Columbia, Missouri, calling someone a "poo-poo-head" was a very powerful high provocation. Although we never conducted the relevant experiment, it seems unlikely that this specific operationalization of high provocation would have worked as well on college students. Does this mean that "provocation effects" on preschoolers do not generalize to college students? In our view, the answer is "yes" *only* if one is foolish enough to expect specific operationalizations (e.g., poo-poo-head) of conceptual variables (e.g., provocation) to generalize. The fact is, provocation effects on aggression (at a conceptual level) generalize across age, sex, culture, and a wide range of additional person and situation characteristics. Obviously, the specific operationalization must fit the participants and the context in which a study (or an intervention) is conducted. This applies to measures of aggression as well. The best measures of naturalistic aggression for 6-year-olds are different from the best measures of naturalistic adulthood aggression. Physical abuse of one's spouse or partner is an appropriate measure for adults but clearly is not appropriate for children.

There are four additional principles that we deem essential to understanding human behavior in general and media violence research in particular.

Laboratory Paradigms Are Valid

The validity of laboratory research paradigms in psychology has passed so many logical and empirical tests that they can be generally accepted as having both high internal and external validity. For example, different laboratory measures of aggression correlate positively with each other and tend to respond to the influences of other aggression-inducing variables in the same way (Carlson, Marcus-Newhall, & Miller, 1989). Similarly, variables that predict real-life aggression and violence have the same effect on laboratory-measured aggression (Anderson & Bushman, 1997). Some of these studies show that situational variables known to increase aggression and violence in the real world have the same type of effect on laboratory aggression. Such variables include provocation, alcohol, the visible presence of a weapon, and media violence. Still other studies show that people who are highly aggressive or violent in real life also display heightened aggression on laboratory measures of aggression. Examples include people who score high on indicators of psychopathic characteristics, hypermasculinity, trait aggression, and Type A personality, to name just a few.

A more recent example involves the psychiatric diagnosis of *intermit-*

tent explosive disorder (IED; McCloskey, Berman, Noblett, & Coccaro, 2006). The IED diagnosis includes a number of criteria, such as (a) verbal or physical aggression toward other people, animals, or property occurring twice weekly on average for one month *or* three episodes involving physical assault or destruction of property over a one-year period; (b) the degree of aggressiveness expressed is grossly out of proportion to the provocation or any precipitating psychosocial stressors. These researchers brought 56 individuals diagnosed with this disorder into a lab setting, along with 56 healthy controls (no history of any psychiatric disorders), 33 DSM-IV Axis I controls (people with a diagnosed Axis I disorder but without an IED or Axis II disorder), and 22 DSM-IV Axis II controls (people with a diagnosed Axis II personality disorder, but not IED). All individuals completed a large number of interviews, questionnaires, and a standard laboratory task for measuring aggressive behavior. The aggression task that was used is a variant of the task used in our Study 1; it is described in more detail later. This task involves choosing a level of punishment (electric shocks) to be given to an opponent on each of a series of reaction time contests. Not surprising, those with a history of aggression and violence (that is, the intermittent explosive disorder participants) also were the most aggressive on this laboratory task (e.g., 91% higher than the normal control participants), just as expected from a valid laboratory measure of aggression.

Aggression Is Best Understood When Viewed as Existing Along a Severity Continuum

Some scholarly domains treat various forms of aggression and violence as though they are qualitatively different and therefore are subject to different principles and influences. We gain considerable explanatory and predictive power by viewing aggression as a fairly homogeneous construct that can vary in severity from mild to extremely severe. Indeed, the best single childhood predictor of aggression and violence at later ages is aggression in childhood, even though the specific forms of aggression change with age (Anderson & Huesmann, 2003).

The Effects of Some Risk Factors Accrue Over Time

Some environmental risk factors for human aggression, such as poor parenting, have cumulative effects that sometimes don't emerge until years after the initial exposure. This is similar to the fact that relatively few teens or young adults die from cigarette-induced lung cancer (relative to smokers in their 50s and 60s).

A General Understanding of Human Aggression Requires a General Perspective

To truly understand the development, execution, prevalence, and distribution of aggression and violence, we need a model that can take into account many factors ranging from biological to cultural and must be informed by relevant theories from developmental, social, cognitive, abnormal, and personality psychology. In a later section we describe such a model. First, we briefly review prior media violence research.

Prior Violent Television and Film Research

As noted earlier, a number of narrative and meta-analytic reviews of television and film violence effects on aggression have appeared over the years. In addition, several expert panels convened by various federal agencies have examined the television and film violence research and issued reports (e.g., Anderson et al., 2003; National Commission on the Causes and Prevention of Violence, 1969; National Institute of Mental Health, 1982; U.S. Surgeon General, 1972). The main conclusion, even from reviews as early as 1969, is that exposure to television violence is a significant risk factor for aggression and violence. That is, exposure to media violence causes an increase in the likelihood of aggression in at least some significant portion of the population.

Examples of Cross-Section Correlational Studies

Cross-sectional studies have consistently found that current physical aggression, verbal aggression, and aggressive thoughts of young people are positively correlated with the amount of television and film violence they regularly watch. Studies reporting significant correlations have used a variety of research methods and measures of aggression, and have examined youngsters of varying ages and cultures (e.g., Huesmann & Eron, 1986).

In some studies, the aggression measure involved physically aggressive acts serious enough to fit the definition of violence. For example, McIntyre and Teevan (1972) surveyed over 2,000 junior and senior high school students in Maryland. Each reported on a variety of aggressive behaviors, including fights at school and serious encounters with the law. Each also was asked to list four favorite TV programs, which were subsequently analyzed for violent content. The aggressive behavior scores were positively correlated with amount of violent content in favorite television shows.

Similarly, McLeod, Atkin, and Chaffee (1972) studied correlations between "aggressive behavioral delinquency" (fighting, hitting, etc.) and TV violence viewing in a sample of over 600 of Wisconsin and Maryland high school and junior high school students. They found significant positive correlations between TV violence exposure and aggression even after controlling for such variables as sex, IQ, and socioeconomic status.

A study of approximately 1,500 English 12- to 17-year-old males (Belson, 1978) reported 49% more violent acts in the past 6 months by heavy TV violence viewers than by light violence viewers.

Cross-sectional correlations have generally been in the small to moderate range (around $r = 0.20$). They tend to be slightly higher for elementary-school children than for teenagers and adults, particularly when general aggression is assessed. However, significant correlations have been found with adults, and cross-age comparisons are risky when different measures are used to assess media violence exposure and aggression at different ages. Of course, as noted earlier, a measure that is appropriate at one age (e.g., spousal abuse by adults) may be inappropriate for another age.

Examples of Experimental Studies

Experimental studies also consistently find higher levels of aggression and aggression-related variables (e.g., aggressive cognitions) after exposure to violent television shows and films than after nonviolent shows and films. These studies provide the strongest evidence of causal effects, though as discussed earlier, all types of well-conducted studies contribute to the development and testing of causal models. For obvious ethical and practical reasons, most experimental studies are of relatively short duration and therefore examine short-term effects of media violence exposure.

For example, Bjorkqvist (1985) exposed 5- and 6-year-old Finnish children to either violent or nonviolent films. Shortly afterward, two raters observed the children playing together in a room. Children who had just watched the violent film displayed significantly more physical aggression (hitting other children, wrestling, etc.) than those who had watched the nonviolent film.

Similarly, Boyatzis, Matillo, and Nesbitt (1995) exposed elementary school children to an episode of *The Mighty Morphin Power Rangers* (a violent children's show); others were assigned to a no-exposure control condition. Behavioral observations of aggression during free play revealed that those who had watched the violent show displayed significantly more aggressive acts (seven times more) than control condition children.

Two related experiments demonstrated that exposure to media violence can lead to increased aggression by teenage boys in juvenile detention facilities. In a study in Belgium, Leyens, Camino, Parke, and Berkowitz

(1975) assigned boys in two cottages to see violent films every night for five nights while boys in the other two cottages saw nonviolent films. Each evening, after the films, the boys were observed for a period of time and were rated for their frequency of hitting, choking, slapping, and kicking their cottage mates. Those who were exposed to the violent films engaged in significantly more physical assaults ($p < 0.025$) on their cottage mates (p levels < 0.05 are generally considered "significant"). Parke, Berkowitz, Leyens, West, and Sebastian (1977) found similar effects with American youth in a minimum-security penal institution for juvenile offenders, on an overall measure of interpersonal attacks (physical or verbal).

College students have also been shown to be susceptible to television and film violence effects. Furthermore, there is evidence that emotionally or physically excited viewers are especially apt to be aggressively stimulated by violent scenes. For example, Geen and O'Neal (1969) found that college student participants who had been provoked by another student and who were also exposed to loud noise (thus increasing arousal) shocked their provocateur significantly more intensely ($p < 0.01$) after they had watched a film of a prizefight than after they had seen a film of a track meet. Similarly, Bushman (1995) found that college students who scored high on trait aggressiveness showed a bigger media violence exposure effect on subsequent aggression than did low trait aggressive participants.

There is also evidence that combining sex and violence in entertainment media is a particularly potent combination. Donnerstein and Berkowitz (1981) found that combining violent portrayals with sexual stimulation led male viewers to be more physically assaultive (electric shocks) toward females who had previously provoked them.

Examples of Longitudinal Studies

Because of their expense, difficulty, and time frame, longitudinal studies of television and film violence are relatively rare. However, those that have been done generally find that early exposure to violent television leads to later aggression, even after controlling for aggressiveness at the earlier time. There is also some evidence that aggressiveness at the earlier time predicts amount of media violence consumption at a later time, but this link is considerably weaker.

Leonard Eron and colleagues began the earliest major study of this type in 1960, with a representative sample of 856 youth in Columbia County, New York. A key finding was that a boy's exposure to media violence at age 8 was significantly related to his aggressive behavior 10 years later at age 18, after he graduated from high school (Eron, Huesmann, Lefkowitz,

& Walder, 1972; Lefkowitz, Eron, Walder, & Huesmann, 1977). This longitudinal effect remained significant when other potentially important factors were statistically controlled. It is interesting that the opposite was not true: boys who were most aggressive at age 8 did not watch more violent TV at age 18. Across an even longer time span, the boys who had watched the most violent TV at age 8 were the most likely to have engaged in violent criminal behavior by age 30 (Huesmann, 1986). Perhaps surprising, girls' television viewing habits at age 8 did not predict later aggression, a finding that has been contradicted by a number of later studies.

A second longitudinal study, commissioned by the NBC television company, studied boys and girls ages 7 to 16 from two Midwestern cities (Milavsky, Kessler, Stipp, & Rubens, 1982). They examined the effects of television violence on aggression by using measures that included serious physical aggression and delinquency. The youths were surveyed up to five times during a 3-year period (1970-1973). The longitudinal correlations between aggressive behavior at one point in time and TV violence viewing at an earlier time were calculated, while statistically controlling for earlier aggression. Most of these lagged correlations were positive, though only a few were statistically significant. Though the authors concluded that there was little evidence of a TV violence effect, that conclusion has been hotly contested on methodological and interpretational grounds. For example, these predictive analyses were based on subsamples from which the research team had deleted the data of many of the most aggressive children (25% of boys and 16% of girls in the initial sample), because they supposedly had not reported their TV viewing accurately. Given that highly aggressive youths appear to be more likely than others to be aggressively stimulated by violent scenes, it may well be that discarding these data artificially decreased the reported effects. Other methodological problems also seem to have biased the results against finding any deleterious effects (Kenny, 1984).

Two more recent longitudinal studies are also instructive. Huesmann et al. (2003) reported the results of a 15-year study of more than 300 U.S. participants who had initially been interviewed while in elementary school, and re-interviewed when they were in their early 20s. The researchers found significant positive correlations between television violence viewing during childhood and a composite measure of aggression (physical, verbal, and indirect) during young adulthood, for both men ($r = 0.21$, $n = 153$, $p < 0.01$) and women ($r = 0.19$, $n = 176$, $p < 0.01$). The lagged correlations remained significant when the outcome examined was restricted to physical aggression or violence ($rs = 0.17$ and 0.15, respectively). The effects of childhood exposure to TV violence on adulthood aggression remained significant even when statistical controls for parents' education and children's achievement were employed. It is interesting that other analyses found that high aggressiveness during childhood did not lead to frequent viewing of television violence later in life.

The other recent longitudinal study examined effects of TV habits in adolescence and early adulthood on later violent behavior (Johnson, Cohen, Smailes, Kasen, & Brook, 2002). Total amount of television watching (not the amount of violent TV viewing) was assessed at ages 14 and 22. As noted elsewhere, in analyzing total time watching TV rather than time watching *violent* TV, the study probably underestimated the true effect of violent television exposure on later aggressive behavior (Anderson & Bushman, 2002b). Despite this, one main result was that TV exposure at age 14 significantly predicted assault and fighting behavior at 16 or 22 years of age, even after controlling statistically for family income, parental education, verbal intelligence, childhood neglect, neighborhood characteristics, peer aggression, and school violence. Furthermore, TV exposure at age 22 significantly predicted assault and fighting behavior at age 30. This is the first longitudinal study to demonstrate potentially harmful effects of viewing television violence by older adolescents and young adults (albeit indirectly, because of the measure of TV viewing).

Summary of Prior Violent Television and Film Research

Briefly, the large and diverse research literature on the effects of exposure to television and film violence is amazingly consistent in its findings. Of course, there are some studies that fail to find significant effects. And of course, some studies are better methodologically than others. But the bottom line is that overall, regardless of primary research method (e.g., experimental, cross-sectional, longitudinal), the evidence strongly points to a significant deleterious effect of violent media on aggression and aggression-related variables. Several meta-analyses bear out this conclusion. For example, Paik and Comstock (1994) reported an average effect size of $r = 0.32$ for experiments in which the outcome measure was classified as physical violence against a person (based on 71 independent tests). For cross-sectional correlational studies of physical aggression against a person (200 independent tests), these same authors reported an average effect size of $r = 0.20$. The only meta-analytic analysis specifically focused on longitudinal effects (Anderson & Bushman, 2002c) also found a significant effect based on 42 independent tests with over 5,000 total participants, $r = 0.17$. In sum, the effects are quite reliable and are between the small to medium range in size (Cohen, 1988) or medium to large range (Hemphill, 2003), depending on whose labels one wishes to use. However, regardless of the label, such effects are large enough to be considered important and of practical significance, as we discuss in a later section.

Prior Violent Video Game Research

The first comprehensive narrative review of the violent video game literature was published by Dill and Dill (1998). They found sufficient evidence of negative effects, similar to the much larger television/film research, to warrant concern by parents, child advocates, and public policy makers. The first comprehensive meta-analytic review (Anderson & Bushman, 2001) yielded results that confirmed this concern. Specifically, Anderson and Bushman found that, across studies, exposure to violent video games was significantly associated with increases in aggressive behavior, aggressive cognition, aggressive affect, and physiological arousal. Furthermore, they found a significant negative association with helping or prosocial behavior. The effect sizes were sufficiently large to warrant concern and were of about the same magnitude regardless of whether the studies used experimental or correlational methods. The effect sizes did not systematically vary by age of participant. More recent meta-analyses (e.g., Anderson, 2004; Anderson, Carnagey, Flanagan, Benjamin, Eubanks, & Valentine, 2004) have yielded somewhat stronger effects, especially for studies with better research methodologies.

Examples of Cross-Section Correlational Studies

Most studies of violent video game effects fall into two types, experimental and cross-section correlational. The best correlational studies share at least three common characteristics: adequate sample size (at least 200),[1] a reliable measure of exposure to violent video games, and a reliable measure of aggression or of an aggression-related variable (e.g., aggressive cognitions). Although the earliest published correlational study of video game effects on aggression was published in 1984 (Dominick), the first one to contain all three of the above-mentioned characteristics didn't appear until 2000 (Anderson & Dill, Study 1). In that study, Anderson and

---

[1] A sample size of 200 is needed to have sufficient power to detect effects of the size typically found in this literature (Anderson & Bushman, 2001). Of course, the "too-small" sample size problem can be effectively handled by combining the results of several similar, well-conducted studies by meta-analytic techniques.

Dill asked their college student participants to list their favorite video games (up to 5), and to indicate how much violence was in each game and how often they had played it in the past. These violence ratings and frequency scores were used to calculate an exposure to violent video games score. The participants also completed measures of aggressive personality (59 items such as "I easily fly off the handle with those who don't listen or understand"), aggressive delinquent behavior (8 items such as "attacked someone with the idea of seriously hurting or killings him/her"), and time spent playing any type of video game. The result of primary interest was a significant positive correlation between exposure to violent video games and self-reported aggressive delinquent behavior, $r = 0.46$, $p < 0.001$. That study also found that the violent video game effect on aggression remained significant even when time spent playing any type of video game, aggressive personality, and sex were statistically controlled. These additional controls ruled out several alternative explanations of the violent video game effect, and thus added considerable strength to the causal theory linking violent media exposure to aggression.

The first published correlational studies with children and with all three above-mentioned characteristics didn't appear until 2004, when two such studies were published. Krahé and Möller (2004) had their sample of eighth-graders in Germany indicate how often they played each of 25 popular video games. Expert adult gamers rated each game on violent content. The violence ratings and frequency scores were used to calculate a video game violence exposure score. Participants also completed an "endorsement of physical aggression norms" scale (7 items such as "To kick and push a person who has made one really angry is OK"). One primary finding was a significant positive correlation between video game violence exposure and endorsement of physical aggression norms, $r = 0.30$, $p < 0.01$.

Gentile et al. (2004), studying eighth and ninth graders in the United States, measured exposure to violent video games in much the same way as Anderson and Dill (2000). They also measured trait hostility, fights at school, and amount of time spent playing any type of video game. They reported significant correlations between video game violence exposure and trait hostility ($r = 0.21$, $p < .001$), arguments with teachers ($r = 0.20$, $p < .001$), and physical fights ($r = 0.32$, $p < 0.001$). They also reported that the violent video game effect on physical fights remained significant even after statistically controlling for sex, trait hostility, and overall amount of video game play. Finally, Gentile et al. found that the amount of time spent playing video games uniquely predicted lower grades, whereas video game violence exposure did not. Anderson and

Dill (2000) reported similar academic results with their college student population.

Examples of Experimental Studies

The best experimental studies also share several characteristics: adequate sample size (about 200 for aggressive behavior studies), violent and non-violent games equated on potentially confounding dimensions (e.g., difficulty),[2] violent and nonviolent games that are truly violent and nonviolent (respectively), and a clear and valid measure of aggression or aggression-related variables assessed for the game-playing participant. Though these characteristics might seem obvious, a number of experimental studies (published and unpublished) do not have all four. Many have small samples. Some present no evidence that the violent and nonviolent games are equated on difficulty or other potentially confounded dimensions. A few (mostly unpublished) have used games that include violence in the non-violent condition, and games with relatively little violence in the violent condition. Still others have used self-reports of past aggression as the dependent variable measure of aggressive behavior.[3]

Although the first published experimental study of violent video games appeared in 1985 (Graybill, Kirsch, & Esselman), the first that contained all four of these high-quality characteristics appeared in 2000 (Anderson & Dill, Study 2). Their college student participants were randomly assigned to play either a violent or nonviolent game. The games were matched on several important dimensions, by selection based on pilot data and by statistical controls used in the main experiment. For example, the two games produced the same levels of physiological arousal (heart rate, blood pressure). Other controlled dimensions were game difficulty, excitement, and frustration. Participants played their assigned games and completed measures of aggressive cognition (a word speed reading task) and of aggressive behavior (a standard competitive game involving the setting of punishment levels for one's opponent). The results were that

---

[2] Such equating can be done by selecting games based on pilot testing or by measuring the to-be-controlled characteristic during the main study and statistically controlling for it.

[3] Such trait aggression measures are appropriately used as measures of aggression in correlational and longitudinal studies but cannot be seen as valid aggression measures in a short-term experimental context. Why should playing a violent video game for 20 minutes in an experiment increase aggression committed prior to starting the experiment? At best, such trait aggression measures in experimental contexts might be used as some type of cognitive measure of aggressive thought processes (Anderson & Bushman, 2001), but better aggressive thought measures exist for experimental contexts (see Table 2.2).

playing a violent video game increased aggressive cognition and aggressive behavior.

Other experimental studies with college students also have found that brief exposure to video game violence increases aggressive behavior, even when the comparison nonviolent game is essentially the same on all relevant dimensions except violence. For example, Carnagey and Anderson (2005) reprogrammed the violent racing game *Carmageddon 2* so that in one condition all the violence was removed. The main result was that those who had been randomly assigned to play the original violent version of the game for 20 minutes behaved more aggressively toward an opponent on a subsequent task (about 51% higher) than those who had initially played the nonviolent version of the game.

To date, there have been no published experimental studies with children that also contain all four of the quality characteristics outlined earlier. However, several smaller scale experiments with children, young adolescents, or both have been conducted over the years. One of the best such studies that focused on aggressive behavior as the outcome measure was reported by Irwin and Gross (1995). Second-grade boys were randomly assigned to play one of two exciting video games, either a violent one (*Double Dragon*, which involves two martial arts heroes fighting to save a friend) or a nonviolent one (*Excitebike*, which involves racing a motorcycle around, over, and through obstacles in a race against the clock). After learning how to control the assigned game, each participant played the game for 20 minutes. Each boy then went to a play room, and played with another boy for about 15 minutes. Behavior was videotaped and coded by coders who were unaware of what game the participant had played. The average number of physically aggressive behaviors was more than twice as high in the violent game condition (11.75) than in the nonviolent game condition (5.25).

Longitudinal Studies

To date there are no major longitudinal studies that specifically focus on violent video game effects, though there are three that are relevant and one that deserves especially careful scrutiny. Slater, Henry, Swaim, and Anderson (2003) surveyed sixth- and seventh-grade students from 20 middle schools across the United States on four occasions over a 2-year period. The media violence measure assessed the frequency of watching action films, playing video games involving firing a weapon, and visiting Internet sites that describe or recommend violence. A composite aggressiveness measure included aggressive cognitions, values, and behavior. Control variables included gender, sensation seeking (a personality trait involving the person's preference for exciting versus quiet activities and environments), general use of the Internet, and age. Media-violence exposure at one point in time was positively (and significantly) related to aggressiveness at a later point in time even after statistically controlling for earlier aggressiveness and various other aggression-related variables. It is interesting that the longitudinal effect of early aggressiveness on later use of violent media was not statistically significant once average level of aggressiveness was statistically controlled. In other words, these results are consistent with the hypothesis that early exposure to violent media (including violent video games) causes an increase in later aggressiveness. The results are inconsistent with the alternative hypothesis that the frequently observed relationship between media violence and aggression is merely the result of "naturally" aggressive children gravitating toward violent entertainment media.

Ihori, Sakamoto, Kobayashi, and Kimura (2003) studied Japanese fifth and sixth graders at two points in time separated by 4 to 5 months, measuring overall video-game exposure (rather than exposure to violent video games). They found that amount of exposure to video games at the initial time period was positively (and significantly) related to later levels of violent physical behavior after controlling for initial time period violent behavior. Again, this study's results are consistent with the hypothesis of video game violence as cause.

However, because neither of these two longitudinal studies specifically focused on violent video game effects, neither has all of the desired features needed to draw strong longitudinal conclusions about effects of violent video games on aggression. Nonetheless, they are suggestive.

Robinson, Wilde, Navracruz, Haydel, and Varady (2001) tested a media use intervention that combined education about the effects of violence with a counterattitudinal intervention and parental monitoring. One of two similar elementary schools was randomly chosen to participate in the intervention while the other served as a control. The intervention consisted of 18 classroom lessons over a 6-month period. The lessons included elements of media education and attitude interventions. The children were encouraged to not watch TV or films or play video games for a "TV Turnoff" period of 10 days. The children also were encouraged to create and follow a video-entertainment budget of 7 hours per week. Newsletters enlisted parents' support in helping their children achieve these goals. Aggressive behavior was assessed in several ways. Peers were asked to report on the participants' aggressive behavior before the intervention (September) and again 7 months later (April). Furthermore, physical and verbal aggression on the playground was assessed for 60% of the children. Also, parents were interviewed about their child's aggressive and delinquent behavior. All four aggression measures yielded relatively lower levels of aggression in April for the intervention participants than for the control participants, though only the peer rating and observed verbal aggression measures were statistically significant. This study combined some elements of experimental and longitudinal designs but is best conceived as a long-term experimental study. Because of the multifaceted nature of the intervention, it is impossible to specify how much of the long-term effect on reducing aggression was the result of a reduction in exposure to violent video games. But again, the results are consistent with the hypothesis that exposure to violent video games plays a causal role in later aggressive behavior.

A final study of interest is also best conceived as a long-term experiment, but it has been characterized by some as a longitudinal study. Williams and Skoric (2005) (based on Williams's dissertation) recruited participants from various Internet sites. Some were randomly assigned to receive a copy of the massively multiplayer online role-playing game (MMORPG, in gamer's lingo) *Asheron's Call 2*, along with a free one-month subscription. Control condition participants received no game. Those who received the game were asked to play it at least five hours a week for one month and to record how much they actually played. Both before the one-month period and afterward, participants were asked to indicate whether they had had at least one argument with a friend and at least one argument with a spouse, boyfriend, or girlfriend. The results were that there was no significant difference between the two groups on change in percentage of participants who had arguments. However, as mentioned earlier this study was plagued with methodological and theoretical problems. For example, a large percentage of participants dropped out of the study (21% in the game condition, 27% in the control condition), effectively ruining it as an experimental design. That is, the *final* sample cannot be seen as having been randomly assigned to condition because such high dropout rates mean that there was much *self-selection* out of (and therefore into) the different groups.

Another major problem is that over 30% of the participants in the game condition did not play the game the minimum number of hours (20), whereas one reported playing almost 300 hours. This negates one of the primary benefits of true experimental studies, which is that participants within each experimental condition are exposed to the same level of the treatment variable.

Yet another major flaw in this study is that there is no evidence that participants in the game condition actually spent more time playing violent video games during the study period than those who remained in the control condition; perhaps those who actually played *Asheron's Call 2* simply played that game instead of their usual violent games, while those in the control condition continued to play their usual amount of violent games—just not *Asheron's Call 2*. Thus, another of the hallmarks of a true experiment—control over the independent variable—does not characterize this study.

Furthermore, it is theoretically unclear whether one should expect massively multiplayer online role-playing games to increase aggression, either in the short term or over time, because they typically involve more cooperation, planning, and social interaction and less violence than the typical shooting and fighting games used in other video game research. Along these same lines, the average age (27.7) and the vast age range (14 to 68) are problematic in a study looking for change in arguing behavior (which, by the way, is not modeled or practiced in violent video games) over a one-month time period.

Finally, another devastating flaw is that the researchers included no true measure of aggression. Arguments with friends and partners rarely constitute aggression. When they do include true aggression, they are typically characterized by verbal aggression. Violent video games typically model physical aggression, not verbal aggression. Therefore, we would not expect them to have much effect on verbal aggression. Furthermore, by only asking participants to self-report whether or not they had been involved in arguments (yes or no), there was no way for this study to measure increases in antisocial behaviors. If one had been involved in an argument at the beginning of the study and also at the end, this study would have only been able to show no change.

In sum, though this study was a well-intentioned attempt to address key hypotheses, the problems we've noted here (some of which were beyond the control of the researchers), as well as several others of a more technical nature, render it wholly uninformative. Even more unfortunate is that some commentators seem to overlook these critical flaws, calling this study "the best study so far," and then claiming that "there's no solid evidence that video games are bad for people, and they may be positively good" (Economist, 2005). Although we certainly agree that many nonviolent video games may have many positive effects, this type of unscientific opining does little to advance scientific understanding; it appears instead to advocate for a position one hopes to be true rather than being responsive to the accumulated scientific data across studies.

Summary of Prior Violent Video Game Research

Meta-Analytic Overview

There have been many studies of violent video games other than the ones briefly described in the prior sections. Populations sampled include children, adolescents, and young adults. Although few studies have all of the characteristics necessary for drawing firm conclusions from them individually, many of them suffer primarily from a small sample size. This is a problem easily handled by meta-analysis techniques. One recent meta-analysis specifically examined the violent video game effects on children (Anderson, 2003). The results showed that, across studies, video game violence exposure is positively associated with aggressive behavior, aggressive affect, and aggressive cognition, and negatively associated with helping or prosocial behavior. There were not enough studies of physiological arousal in children to permit a meta-analysis.

The most recent meta-analysis of this research domain compared the effects found in studies with the best methodological features to effects found in studies that had at least one serious potential methodological weakness (other than sample size) (Anderson et al., 2004). (See Appendix 1 for a list of the methodological weaknesses identified.) The results appear in Figure 2.1. As can be seen, studies with better methods yielded larger average effect sizes than those with at least one weakness for each of the five types of outcome variables. And in each case, the average effect size is significantly different from zero. Exposure to violent video games is associated with increases in aggressive behavior, aggressive affect, aggressive cognition, physiological arousal, and with decreases in prosocial behavior.

Contextualized Overview

Although a meta-analysis is an excellent way to summarize a research domain, by itself it does not adequately convey the types of studies that are summarized by it or some of the issues warranting further attention. Measures of aggressive affect (e.g., state hostility, anger), prosocial behavior (e.g., donating pennies or candy), and physiological arousal (e.g., heart rate, blood pressure) are fairly obvious and need no further discussion. However, the wide range of aggressive behavior and cognition used in various video game studies is worth detailing. Tables 2.1 and 2.2 list measures of aggressive behavior and aggressive cognition that have been used in violent video game studies. The range in each is quite impressive.

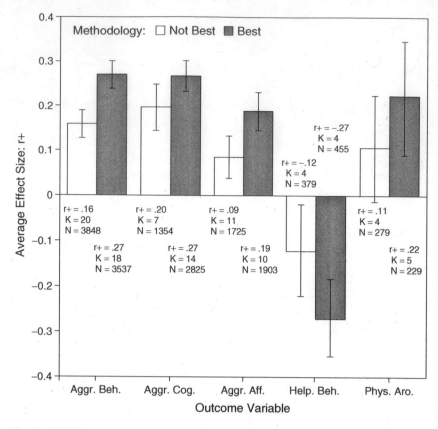

Figure 2.1 Effects of violent video games on aggressive behavior, cognition, and affect; helping behavior; and physiological arousal by methodological quality. "Not Best" studies have at least 1 of 9 specific methodological weaknesses described in Appendix 1. "Best" studies have none. r+ = average effect size. K = number of independent samples. N = total number of participants. Vertical capped bars are the upper and lower 95% confidence intervals. Adapted from Anderson et al. (2004), with permission from Elsevier Inc.

These two types of measures are, in our view, particularly important in the study of media violence effects, especially violent video game effects. Aggressive behavior is important because it is, after all, the focal point of the whole media violence issue. The range of measures used to assess violent video game effects on aggressive behavior helps establish the generality and importance of this issue. Aggressive cognition is important because theoretically it is the main route that leads from the relatively short-lived effects of one brief exposure to violent video games to the long-term effects of repeated exposure. Indeed, the reason that many exist-

TABLE 2.1   Measures of aggressive behavior used in violent video game studies

Punishment level for opponent (e.g., aversive noise blasts)
Hitting, kicking, punching, biting . . .
Fights at school
Physical assault (teachers, peers, parents)
Robbery
Verbal aggression
Teacher ratings of aggression
Peer ratings of aggression
Parent ratings of aggression
Self-report of aggression
Juvenile delinquency
Relational aggression

TABLE 2.2   Measures of aggressive cognition used in violent video game studies

Reading reaction times to aggressive and nonaggressive words
Hostile attribution biases in response to hypothetical conflict situations (a tendency to attribute hostile motives to an individual who may have accidentally, not intentionally, harmed someone else)
Aggressive concepts contained in story completions
Trait aggression/trait hostility measures when used in an experimental study
Word completion (e.g., h_t can be completed to form hit, hat, hut, hot)
Speed of recognition of various facial expression (e.g., happy vs. angry faces)
Implicit association test (aggressive self-concept)
Aggressive attitudes, norms, and beliefs

ing experiments on violent video game effects have attempted to control for excitement and arousal, or frustration and anger, is not because these other potential effects of violent game content are unimportant, but because testing the independent effect of violent video game content on aggressive thinking (or cognition) is so very important. The next section on the General Aggression Model discusses this issue in more detail.

3

The General Aggression Model

As discussed earlier, there have been several closely related theoretical models to help explain and predict the effects of media violence exposure on viewers. Furthermore, there has been a great deal of research to support many of them. For example, social learning theory (Bandura, 1973), social cognitive theory (Bandura, 1986), cognitive neoassociation models (e.g., Berkowitz, 1984, 1990, 1993), social information processing models (e.g., Crick & Dodge, 1994), affective aggression models (e.g., Geen, 1990), script theory (e.g., Huesmann, 1986), excitation transfer models (e.g., Zillmann, 1983), and cultivation theory (e.g., Gerbner, Gross, Morgan, & Signorielli, 1982) have all been used to help describe the effects of media violence exposure on aggression with some success (for a brief review, see Carnagey & Anderson, 2003). However, two aspects have been missing. First, the field of human aggression has needed a unified theoretical model that integrates the empirically valuable aspects of each of the more specific theoretical models, including models that are narrowly focused on media violence effects. Second, most of the specific models have not been explicitly developmental in nature or have not been integrated with advances in developmental theories.

The General Aggression Model (see Anderson & Bushman, 2002a; Anderson & Carnagey, 2004; Anderson & Huesmann, 2003) was developed to integrate key ideas from earlier models: social learning theory and related social cognitive theory concepts (e.g., Bandura, 1971, 1973; Bandura, Ross, & Ross, 1961, 1963; Mischel 1973; Mischel & Shoda, 1995), Berkowitz's cognitive neoassociationist model (1984, 1990, 1993), Dodge and Cricks's social information-processing model (e.g., Crick & Dodge,

1994; Dodge & Crick, 1990), Geen's affective aggression model (1990), Huesmann's script theory (Huesmann, 1986), and Zillmann's excitation transfer model (1983). The General Aggression Model thus helps solve the first problem, and will be described in more detail below. This monograph further proposes integrating a developmental risks and resilience approach into the General Aggression Model. Finally, three studies that are guided by the General Aggression Model will show its value for creating testable, developmentally relevant hypotheses.

General Aggression Model: Overview

Figure 3.1 presents the General Aggression Model in its broadest view. The General Aggression Model distinguishes between variables and processes that operate in the current situation (proximate causes and processes) and those that exert their influence over a long period of time (distal causes and processes). As illustrated in Figure 3.1, two types of distal factors (called biological and environmental modifiers) influence proximate factors (person and situation variables). Basically, distal risk factors for aggression are those that facilitate proximate factors that directly increase aggression or that decrease normal inhibitions against aggression. For the most part, distal factors influence the individual's personal preparedness to aggress, that is, aggressive personality.

A Knowledge Structures Approach

Like several of its predecessors, the General Aggression Model is based on the assumption that human memory, thought, and decision processes can be represented as a complex associative network of nodes representing cognitive concepts and emotions. Experience leads to the development of links among elemental nodes. Nodes that are simultaneously activated gain associative strength from that activation. Nodes with similar meaning are also linked. Concepts that are strongly interconnected are known as *knowledge structures*. The activation level (or accessibility) of a simple node or a more complex knowledge structure at any time is determined both by how many links to it have been activated and by the strength of associations among the activated links. When total activation is sufficiently high (i.e., above threshold), the knowledge structure is activated and used. However, even when a knowledge structure is not fully activated, it can still influence other cognitive and emotional processes, decisions, and behavior. In such cases, the knowledge structure is said to have been *primed*. It is important to note that an activated (or highly accessible) knowledge

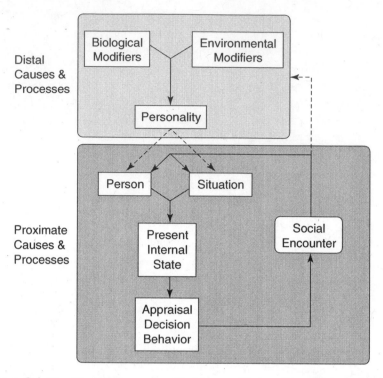

Figure 3.1 The General Aggression Model: overall view. From Anderson & Carnagey (2004). Copyright 2004 by Guilford Press. Reprinted by permission.

structure is not necessarily conscious, in keeping with current theories of cognition, decision making, and consciousness.

Figure 3.2 displays two such knowledge structures and their links for illustrative purposes. In Figure 3.2 line thickness represents association strength; distance represents dissimilarity of meaning. One knowledge structure is an aggression concept representing a schema that includes "gun" as a central concept. The retaliation script represents another type of knowledge structure (i.e., a "script") that includes decision rules and actions to take when intentionally provoked. The linkages between these two knowledge structures illustrate how network associations can activate specific behavioral scripts. Activating the gun schema will also tend to activate the retaliation script by its associations with "pain," "anger," and "use gun." Once the retaliation script is primed it becomes a likely tool for interpreting an ambiguous situation involving some type of potential provocation such as ridicule, and thereby increases the likelihood of retaliation.

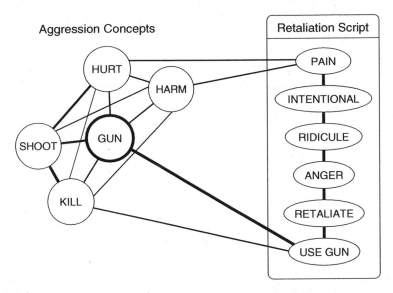

Figure 3.2 Simplified associative network with aggression concepts and a retaliation script. From Anderson, Benjamin, & Bartholow, 1998. Copyright 1998 by the American Psychological Society. Reprinted by permission.

In general, knowledge structures influence perception at multiple levels, from basic visual patterns to complex behavioral sequences. They guide people's interpretations and behavioral responses to their environment. They can contain affective states, behavioral programs, and beliefs. They are essentially learned through biosocial interactions with the environment. With high usage or practice, a particular script can become automated, so that it is activated easily, quickly, and without awareness. This knowledge structure approach highlights the role of learning in the development of aggressive (and nonaggressive) individuals. From this social-cognitive approach, personality is the sum of a person's knowledge structures (cf. Mischel & Shoda, 1995; Sedikides & Skowronski, 1990); their development and construction is based on life experiences, in conjunction with biological influences. Individuals differ in how they construe and respond to their social world, and even the same social event. Of course, situational realities impose constraints on how people construe a given event, but individual differences in the structure, accessibility, and use of underlying knowledge structures create a range of possible construals of any specific event.

The process by which schemas, scripts, and other types of knowledge structure are activated is cognitive but can with repetition become automatic and operate without awareness (Schneider & Shiffrin, 1977; Todorov & Bargh, 2002). Therefore, we can view each life event (including but not limited to social episodes) as a learning trial, leading to the development of well-rehearsed and eventually automatized knowledge structures of various kinds. Thus, the attainment of specific developmental stages (e.g., Piagetian stages) occurs when key knowledge structures have been successfully learned and automatized. And of course, certain knowledge structures cannot be learned until certain other knowledge structures have been automatized.

Proximate Causes and Processes: The Social Episode

Figure 3.3 expands the proximate causes and processes part of the overall model. To date, research on the General Aggression Model has focused mostly on this episodic cycle. Current inputs from the person (e.g., mood, attitudes, personality variables) and the situation (e.g., provocation) combine (additively and interactively) to produce the person's present internal state, represented by affect, cognition, and arousal variables. For example, K. Anderson, Anderson, Dill, and Deuser (1998) found that pain (a situational manipulation) and trait hostility (a person variable) interactively affect aggressive cognitions. Present internal state then influences a host of appraisal and decision processes (see Anderson & Bushman, 2002a, for more detail; see also Anderson, Krull, and Weiner, 1998, for a discussion of general explanation processes). Eventually (sometimes very quickly) an action emerges, which in turn moves the social encounter along to its next cycle, as illustrated by the social encounter box and its link back to person and situation variables. But as the overall model indicates, the results of each social encounter also feed back into the distal causes and processes.

Distal Causes and Processes: Development of Aggressive Personality

Figure 3.4 illustrates some of the key types of personality variables believed to be influenced by a person's history of biosocial interactions. Within the General Aggression Model (and other social-cognitive models) each social episode is seen as another learning trial. What is learned, over time, depends on each individual's life experience, but biological factors also play a key role in multiple ways. For example, biological factors influence one's ability to learn certain types of associations (such as the link between certain misbehaviors and punishment) or one's ability to perform certain kinds of behaviors (and thus success and failure rates).

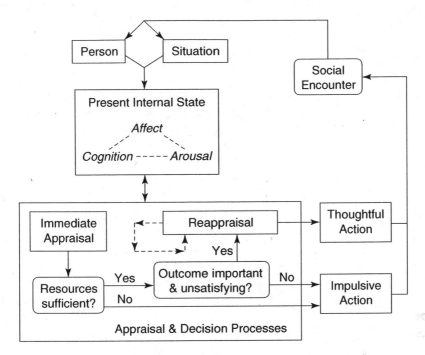

Figure 3.3 Expanded proximate causes and processes: the episodic cycle.

General Aggression Model Summary: Multiple Causes of Aggression

The General Aggression Model highlights the fact that a wide variety of factors influence the development and expression of aggressive tendencies at multiple levels of analysis, from the individual to societal patterns. In this way, it responds to criticisms that have sometimes been leveled at theories attempting to account for the effects of media violence on children—that they do not take into account the various ecological contexts that surround children. Jordan (2004), for example, suggests that theories should be able to account for contextual variables at each of Bronfenbrenner's ecological levels. These include the microsystem (children's day-to-day settings, such as family and school), the mesosystem (relationships between the microsystems), the exosystem (social settings that do not have direct interactions with children but still can affect them such as the parents' workplace and the mass media), and the macrosystem (broad cultural variables, such as history and ethnicity). The General Aggression Model can be used to incorporate variables at each of these levels, and has the added benefit of also being able to use individual difference variables

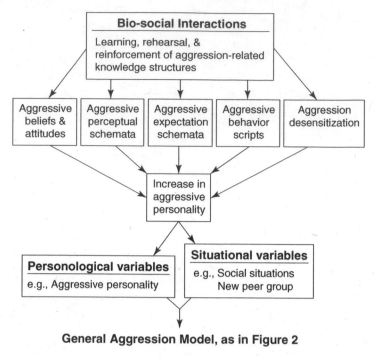

General Aggression Model, as in Figure 2

Figure 3.4 The General Aggression Model: developmental and personality processes. From Anderson & Carnagey (2004). Copyright 2004 by Guilford Press. Reprinted by permission.

when attempting to explain development. Although Jordan suggests that mass media are most appropriately placed at the exosystem level, it is unclear that video games belong here. Because they are an interactive media, they also appear to have direct effects with children (microsystem) as well as influencing relationships between microsystems (such as when children play or talk about video games both in school and at home). It may be that video games could have effects at several ecological levels, although this remains to be tested.

Although the General Aggression Model focuses primarily on the individual in the situation, it is easy to extrapolate the findings to society at large. For example, the easy accessibility of guns (O'Donnell, 1995), global warming (Anderson, Bushman, & Groom, 1997), cultural norms about violence (Nisbett and Cohen, 1996), and widespread exposure to violent entertainment media (Anderson et al., 2003) all are likely to contribute to the high level of violence and aggression in the United States and to differences between societies. The General Aggression Model also accounts for the fact that severe aggressive and violent acts rarely occur unless multiple precipitating *situational instigators* and multiple predis-posing *personal characteristics* converge. The shooters at Columbine High School—who killed 13 people and wounded 23 before killing them-selves—were high consumers of violent media (especially violent video games), but there were numerous other risk factors present as well (e.g., easy availability of guns, feeling persecuted at school, less involved par-ents). Such seems to be the case in most extreme acts of violence. Accord-ing to the General Aggression Model, habitual aggressive tendencies are most likely to develop in children who grow up in environments that rein-force aggression, provide aggressive models, frustrate and victimize them, and teach them that aggression is acceptable and successful. The acquired aggressive scripts, schemas, and beliefs are most likely to produce aggres-sion when situational factors both instigate and disinhibit aggression.

Table 3.1 presents a partial list of situational instigators, personal pre-paredness factors, environmental modifiers, and biological modifiers that have been identified in the wider human aggression arena (Anderson & Huesmann, 2003). Of course, the same environmental stimulus may be both an environmental modifier and a situational instigator, as shown in Table 3.1. Exposure to a violent video game both primes aggression-related knowledge structures in the immediate situation and constitutes an additional learning trial that teaches the viewer beliefs that will have longer-lasting effects. (For more details on the General Aggression Model and related social-cognitive models of aggression, see Anderson & Bush-man, 2002a; Anderson & Carnagey, 2004; Anderson & Huesmann, 2003).

Table 3.1 Proximal and distal risk factors for aggression

Proximal Risk Factors	Distal Risk Factors
Situational instigators	*Environmental modifiers*
Provocation	Family practices
Frustration	Community violence
Pain & discomfort	Culture of violence/hate
Bad mood	Media violence
Social stress	Extreme social environments
Aggressive primes (e.g., media violence)	
Personal preparedness	*Biological modifiers*
Inflated/unstable high self-esteem	Low serotonin
Pro-aggression beliefs	Low arousal
Pro-aggression attitudes	Executive functioning deficits
Hostile world schemas	ADHD
Aggressive scripts	Other genetic factors
Aggression-related goals	

A Focus on Development

Risk and Resilience

The multiple factors approach taken by the General Aggression Model is very similar to recent advances in developmental theories that seek to explain individual differences in development (including the development of aggression) via a risk and resilience perspective (see reviews by Dodge & Petit, 2003; Glantz & Johnson, 1999; Masten & Coatsworth, 1998). A risk and resilience approach focuses on differential life experiences among children that may put them at risk for future maladaptation (risk factors) and on those factors that serve to "protect" children from this risk exposure (protective factors). This approach may help explain why we might see greater effects of media violence on some children than on others. Exposure to media violence is likely to be a "risk factor" for all children. However, some children may have protective factors that reduce, mask, or attenuate the effects of exposure to media violence whereas other children may have additional risk factors that enhance the effects of media violence exposure.

One of the most robust findings in the study of risk and resilience is that of the cumulative risk model (Masten, 2001). The premise behind a cumulative risk model is simple: for every additional risk factor encountered by a child the likelihood of problematic functioning increases (Masten & Wright, 1998; Rutter, 2000; Sameroff & Fiese, 2000). Though simple in premise, the strength in such an approach lies in its acknowledgment that a true challenge to the developmental system comes from the summing or interaction of multiple risk factors, and that this cumulative risk process is greater than any one single risk factor in derailing healthy development (Belsky & Fearon, 2002). Many risk factors for healthy development have been studied, including marital discord, low socioeconomic status (SES), maternal psychological distress, single parent status or divorce, low maternal education, and exposure to violence (Masten, 2001; Masten, Miliotis, Graham-Bermann, Ramirez, & Neemann, 1993; Rutter, 2000), as well as genetic risk factors for psychopathology or aggression (Rutter et al., 1997). Unfortunately for children, there is often comorbidity among risk factors. Risk factors seldom occur in isolation; children experiencing one risk factor frequently experience a variety of other risk factors (Masten, 2001).

Researchers using the risk and resilience approach occasionally find that there are individuals who appear less vulnerable to risk factors than other individuals. This phenomenon, termed *resilience,* refers to the observation that despite experiencing severe adversity, some children display normal or above normal levels of competence across an array of domains

(Masten, Hubbard, Gest, Tellegen, Garmezy, & Ramirez, 1999). Early perspectives on resilience mistakenly labeled such children as stress-resistant or invulnerable. These labels incorrectly implied that there is something special about the child, such as having a hardy constitution that rendered children impervious to stress and adversity (e.g., Anthony, 1974). Current thinking regarding resilience assumes that a successful outcome despite stress exposure arises out of dynamic interactions between the child and the environment (Masten, 2001). That is, the outcome occurs as a result of multiple risk and protective factors—genetic, interpersonal, contextual, and societal—that impinge on the child as well as interact with each other (Sameroff, Seifer, & Bartko, 1997).

A clear finding from studies of resilience is that there are no extraordinary children or circumstances that account for successful development in the context of adversity. Instead, protective factors such as good self-regulation, close relationships with caregivers and other adults, and effective schools are all implicated as factors contributing to resilience processes (Masten & Coatsworth, 1998; Masten & Reed, 2002).

A key issue implied in our discussion of risk and resilience factors, one that is frequently ignored or misunderstood, concerns their additivity versus interactivity. The early claims of stress resistance or hardiness or invulnerability imply a statistically interactive model, in which certain types of children are essentially unaffected by certain types of stressors, whereas other types of children are especially vulnerable. But it now appears that such statistical interactions are relatively rare, and that most children are adversely affected by common risk factors (although it has been argued that this failure to find interactions may be due to methodological constraints rather than by a true absence of interactions; Petit, 2004). In the violence domain, especially when focusing on the most violent behaviors, it is easy to mistakenly assume interactive models because more perpetrators of homicide have multiple risk factors. But we believe that a purely additive model, in which each risk factor incrementally increases the likelihood of aggressive behavior, accounts for the data at least as well as more complex interactive models. Therefore children may not be especially vulnerable to the effects of media violence just by virtue of being children, as some theorists have suggested (e.g., by citing the fantasy-reality distinction or differences in cognitive processing abilities). It may be that there are no "vulnerable" or "immune" populations per se, but instead what makes an individual "vulnerable" is the sum of multiple risk factors or the absence of protective factors, or a combination thereof. It is critical, however, that studies be designed that can compare additive to "transactional" models (Rutter, 2003).

With regard to media violence, our view is that exposure to entertainment media violence is a risk factor for aggressive behavior and other negative outcomes. This is in accordance with current risk models for the development of conduct problems (e.g., Dodge & Petit, 2003; Rutter, 2003; Petit, 2004). In the words of Dodge & Petit (2003, p. 352), for example, this "model proposes that early contexts of disadvantage [i.e., risk factors] place a child at probabilistic risk for later conduct problems and that the path is likely to be indirect." The presence of this single risk factor is not sufficient to cause children to pick up guns and begin shooting people. However, each additional risk factor children have for aggressive behavior (e.g., being bullied, antisocial friends, gang membership, drug use, poverty, history of being abused, access to guns) adds to the risk of that child acting violently. Similarly, each additional protective factor children have (e.g., stable family environment, good school performance, open communication with parents) reduces the risk of violent behavior. Of course, some risk factors may have larger effects than others, just as some protective factors may be more important than others.

In their excellent review of the multiple risk factors for the development of antisocial conduct problems, Dodge & Petit (2003) liken understanding multiple risk factors and the processes they represent to heart disease. Similar to heart disease, one single causal agent of aggressive behavior will never be found. In order to understand development of aggressive behaviors and personality, one must build a model with multiple, diverse risk factors. Multiple factors also suggest that there may be several possible mechanisms and pathways for each risk factor to affect development. The situation is made even more difficult by the fact that many of these risk factors are comorbid and are linked to several other outcomes besides aggression (e.g., hostile attribution bias may lead not only to aggressive behaviors but also to peer rejection, which has been linked to many negative outcomes).

In theory, measuring multiple risk factors at several ecological levels should provide an excellent approach to predicting aggressive behavior, and perhaps even serious violence. In middle childhood and later, aggressive behavior is a fairly rare occurrence. Similarly, a myocardial infarction (heart attack) is a fairly rare occurrence in the population. But the power of a risk factor approach allows us to predict these rare occurrences well. For example, in a longitudinal study of children from 6 months of age until adolescence, problematic infant temperament, low socioeconomic status at birth, early experience of physical abuse, and peer rejection in early elementary school all were shown to be risk factors for adolescent conduct problems (Dodge & Petit, 2003). Children who had none of these risk factors were at low risk for adolescent conduct problems (7%), children who had any one of these were at moderate risk (range 11–30%), whereas children with all four had a significant risk of severe conduct problems in adolescence (57%).

This approach helps in responding to the comment most people make about media violence: "I watched a lot of media violence as a kid, and I never shot anyone." We need to remember that "shooting someone" is a highly extreme and rare behavior. Most people will never engage in such behavior, and exposure to media violence by itself is unlikely to induce extremely violent behavior. Of course, other single risk factors such as growing up in poverty (or easy access to guns) are also unlikely to induce extremely violent behavior in the absence of additional risk factors.

One metaphor for this cumulative risk model is the risk thermometer shown in Figure 3.5 (Gentile & Sesma, 2003).[1] At the lowest end, an individual's behavior is routinely respectful and polite. At the highest end, an individual engages in the ultimate disrespectful behavior of shooting

Shooting or stabbing someone

Hitting with intent to injure

Occasional threats of violence

Pushing and shoving

Occasional violent thoughts/fantasies

Verbally aggressive behavior

Occasional aggressive thoughts/fantasies

Occasional rude behavior

Routinely respectful and polite behavior

Figure 3.5 The risk thermometer. From Gentile & Sesma (2003). Copyright 2003 by Praeger Publishers. Reprinted by permission.

[1] This metaphor is used with the understanding that it is imperfect. For example, this thermometer describes a hierarchy most typical of male aggression, whereas females are more likely to engage in relational rather than physical aggression (e.g., Crick, 1995; Crick & Dodge, 1996). Indeed, the hierarchy might differ somewhat for a variety of subgroup or cultural reasons. It is intended solely to help describe how different risk factors can increase the likelihood of more severe aggressive behaviors, and how protective factors can decrease the likelihood of aggressive behaviors.

someone. Media violence exposure may be able to elevate someone several levels on the risk thermometer, but by itself is not a strong enough effect to move someone from routinely respectful behavior all the way to shooting someone. If, however, an individual starts out with other risk factors for violent behavior, and is already at the verbally aggressive spot on the thermometer, regular exposure to media violence may add enough additional risk to get him or her to start pushing and shoving others around. In addition, the individual may also have several protective factors, which serve to lower the level of aggression.

We do not mean to imply that there are never issues of "vulnerability" for youth. However, we believe that the issues are not as clear as they have been made out to be. For example, it is common to hear people (including some media scholars) say that young children (under age 8) are more "vulnerable" to the effects of media violence because they lack the ability to distinguish between fantasy and reality. In our view, this is a mistaken conclusion drawn from some developmental truths. It is a fact that young children do not understand the concepts of pretend and real the same way that adults do (e.g., Taylor & Flavell, 1984; Malamuth & Impett, 2001). However, it is unclear that this has much, if anything, to do with susceptibility to media effects. For example, adults all "know" that advertisements are fake; yet they still work (Woodward & Denton, 2000). Therefore, an advanced ability to distinguish between fantasy and reality does not seem to be a particularly good moderator of media effects. Furthermore, we know of no studies that have empirically tested this hypothesis in a controlled manner—for example, selecting children of the same chronological age but different conceptual levels in ability to distinguish fantasy from reality, and then measuring the relative effect sizes of media violence on them. But there are many media violence studies with college student participants that have found significant increases in aggression as a result of exposure to cartoonish violent media. Again, neither age nor the associated ability to distinguish between fantasy and reality protect one from media effects.

Developmental Tasks

Nonetheless, numerous researchers have identified age as a variable related to aggression, both in its causes and in the emergence of its displays (Anderson & Huesmann, 2003). As discussed previously, age by itself is not an independent variable with any power of its own. At best, it is a proxy for other variables that may moderate the effects of media violence on aggression. However, advances in developmental theory may provide a new integrative approach to understanding how and why age relates to the effects of media violence on aggressive behavior. This is the developmental tasks approach. In contrast to the risk and resilience approach, which examines individual differences as a method to predict which children will exhibit certain outcomes, the developmental tasks approach is a normative model. Developmental tasks are capacities or skills that are important for concurrent and future adaptation (Gentile & Sesma, 2003; Havighurst, 1949; Sroufe, 1979).

> In developmental psychopathology, adaptation is often defined in terms of developmental tasks. . . . The basic idea is that in order for a person to adapt, there are developmental challenges that must be met. Some arise through biological maturation, others are imposed by families and society, while others arise from the developing self. (Masten & Braswell, 1991, p. 13)

Researchers have used this approach for at least two purposes. First, it provides a set of criteria by which to judge adaptation at any particular point in development. All children within any culture are presumed to face these tasks at some point in development, and therefore these tasks can serve as an indicator from which to infer competence or maladaptation (Masten & Coatsworth, 1998). Second, this approach provides a framework for researchers and practitioners to understand how development unfolds over childhood. For example, the etiology of depression can be studied within such a framework to explain how and where normal development went awry (Cicchetti & Toth, 1998).

The developmental task approach rests on several assumptions. First, there is a hierarchy to the tasks (Sroufe, 1979, 1995). Different issues rise in importance depending on the developmental level of the child. For example, in infancy, the most important task is to form a healthy attachment relationship with a primary caregiver. As can be seen in Table 3.2, this task recedes in importance as other tasks arise.

However, this does not mean that early tasks are irrelevant at later stages. Instead, it is assumed by this approach that development is cumulative and builds on prior adaptation. For example, the degree to which a child is able to form a secure attachment to a primary caregiver has direct implications for how she negotiates the next tasks, such as active exploration of her environment. If a child established a secure attachment relationship in infancy, and this helped her actively explore her environment in the toddler years, then the child is in a good position to deal with issues of self-regulation, which is a major developmental task during the preschool period. Development proceeds in this way, building on past resolutions and negotiations. And of course, the knowledge structure approach exemplified by the General Aggression Model fits this developmental process approach very well.

TABLE 3.2   Examples of developmental tasks

Key Developmental Tasks of Infancy (~0–12 Months)

Attachment to caregiver(s)
Regularity of Patterns
Transition from reflex to voluntary behavior

Key Developmental Tasks of Toddlerhood (~1–2 Years)

Curiosity, exploration, and mastery
Differentiation of self from world
Independence of actions, such as self-care and feeding
Learning of language

Key Developmental Tasks of Early Childhood (~2–5 Years)

Learning behavioral self-control and compliance with external rules
Learning emotional self-control
Learning gender roles and stereotypes

Key Developmental Tasks of Middle Childhood (~6–12 Years)

Learning how to build loyal friendships and to be accepted by peers
Learning social rules and norms
Adjusting to school
Learning the importance of academic achievement and real-world competence
Moral development
Consolidating self-concept (in terms of the peer group)

Key Developmental Tasks of Adolescence (~13–18 Years)

Learning to build intimate and committed friendships/relationships
Adjustment to pubertal changes
Transition to secondary schooling
Develop strong and coherent personal identity

Adapted from Aber & Jones (1997), Masten & Braswell (1991), Sroufe, Cooper, & DeHart (1996), Sroufe, Egeland, & Carlson (1999).

The effects that violent (or other) media may have on children and youth may be very different depending on the age of the child in question. As children face different developmental tasks, media are likely to have a greater or lesser effect depending on the specific issues the children are facing at that time. Gentile & Sesma (2003) have provided a more detailed description of this approach than is possible here. However, the following example provided in that chapter may illuminate the potential utility of this approach.

The answer to the question, "How will this television show/video game/film affect children?" is unlikely to be unidimensional. The effects are likely to differ greatly depending on the developmental stage of the child. Consider the following example taken from a nationally broadcast episode of professional wrestling (*WWF Smackdown*, Oct 7, 1999). Wrestling was selected as an example of media violence here because it is highly watched by children (historically it has been the highest rated show on cable; Keller, 2002), has lots of violence, and poses a major risk (e.g., Tamborini, Skalski, Lachlan, Westerman, Davis, & Smith, 2005).

> A male wrestler, Jeff Jarrett, is angry at his wrestler girlfriend, Miss Kitty, because she lost a wrestling match the previous week. In order to "get back on [his] good side," he requires Miss Kitty to participate in a mud wrestling match. He asks the reigning ladies' champion, Ivory, to stand near the ring to watch. He then announces that the goal of the match is to remove the opponent's shirt and bra in order to win. He then throws Ivory into the mud, to her apparent surprise. Miss Kitty immediately attacks Ivory, removing Ivory's dress. Meanwhile, Jarrett makes comments about women being the lowest form of life and the announcers make lascivious comments about the women's bodies. Ivory eventually removes Miss Kitty's bikini top, "winning" the match. Incensed older women wrestlers arrive to confront Jarrett, who promptly throws them into the mud, while making comments about them being fat old sows. Ultimately, another lady wrestler, Chyna, sneaks up behind Jarrett, and pushes him into the mud. (Gentile & Sesma, 2003, pp. 32-33)

How might children who watch shows like this be affected? The developmental tasks approach provides a framework to understand how the effects may be different for children of different ages.

In infancy, shows like this are unlikely to have much effect, unless the parents watch them so much that it interferes with their ability to respond to and care for the infant. In toddlerhood, when language acquisition is critical, children might learn many derogatory terms their parents would prefer they hadn't. However, children at this age are just beginning to acquire societal norms of behavior. This type of program shows violence as the solution to interpersonal conflict, as well as the "normality" of verbal and physical abuse toward women (particularly, scantily clad women).

In early childhood, where the main developmental tasks are about behavioral self-control, emotional self-control, and learning sex roles, this type of program could have a number of negative effects. Very little self-control is displayed. Words are used to exacerbate the situation, rather than to help solve problems. The episode was derogatory toward women, and the male wielded all the power. Jarrett defined the rules for the contest, and because Ivory was allegedly "tricked" into the ring, there was no reason she needed to comply with Jarrett's rules—yet she did comply with them. Although some could say that women "won" in the end, they did it by continuing the cycle of violence that Jarrett set up. Children at this age may begin to accept the stereotype that women should comply with whatever men say, and that such behaviors are normal and natural.

In middle childhood, the learning of social rules and norms takes on increased importance. Children at this age are likely to learn that physical domination and humiliation of others are acceptable and appropriate methods of interpersonal interaction, especially if they are engaged in a conflict situation. Furthermore, in this example, competence was defined only in terms of one's ability to fight physically (although there was also a subtext of sexuality as female competence).

For adolescents the major developmental task is learning how to have intimate and committed relationships, both same-sex and cross-sex. In this type of show, relationships between men and women are very stereotypical, in that the males have the power and the females are submissive. It also portrays physical aggression between the sexes as acceptable (and sexual).

We do not mean to suggest that watching any single episode of a program is likely to have an immediate, large effect. But both short-term and long-term effects are likely to be different based on the age of the child, and the developmental tasks approach provides a framework for designing and testing hypotheses about the types of effects we might expect at different ages. This approach may also provide a useful way of considering the issue of youth "vulnerability" to the effects of media violence. Rather than simply assuming that children are more generally vulnerable due to their cognitive level or some other factor, it may be that children are most "vulnerable" to being affected along dimensions that parallel the salient developmental tasks for children at different developmental stages. Thus, in terms of the General Aggression Model, developmental stage is one of the personological variables that individuals bring to any situation.

The General Aggression Model, Media Violence, and Aggression

One limitation that risk factor approaches have is that by themselves they tell us little about the mechanisms by which the risk factors may operate or how development unfolds based on their presence or absence (Dodge & Petit, 2003). For this reason, the General Aggression Model is a powerful theoretical advance, because it not only includes the strengths of a developmental risk and resilience approach, but also it posits specific testable pathways of effect based on many previous specific theories. This transactional developmental model proposes that biological, sociocultural, parent, peer, and individual variables interact in the context of the individual's life experiences, which shape that individual's beliefs, attitudes, schemata, scripts, and responses (Figure 3.4). These changes in turn can be considered holistically as an increase in aggressive personality, which changes the contexts into which the individual will enter and the responses the individual will make to those contexts.

The General Aggression Model can be used to interpret the effects of virtually anything the person comes into contact with in his or her environment, including exposure to violent media. Theoretically, violent media can affect all three components of internal state. As noted earlier, the relatively small research literature on violent video games has shown that playing them can temporarily increase aggressive thoughts, aggressive affect, and arousal (Anderson & Bushman, 2001). For example, Anderson & Dill (2000) showed that playing a violent video game increased the relative speed with which the person could read aggression-related words (aggressive thoughts). Similarly, Kirsh (1998) and Bushman & Anderson (2002) found that playing a violent video game subsequently increased hostile interpretations of ambiguous social events (aggressive schemata). Uhlmann and Swanson (2004) found that both habitual exposure and recent brief exposure to violent video games increased automatic self-associations with aggressive traits and actions (aggressive self-schemata). Kirsh, Olczak, and Mounts (2005) reported that brief exposure to a violent video game increased the automatic recognition of aggressive words (aggressive cognition). And as noted earlier, exposure to violent media can reduce arousal to subsequent depictions of violence (physiological desensitization; Carnagey, Anderson, & Bushman, 2007; Linz, Donnerstein, & Adams, 1989; Thomas, Horton, Lippincott, & Drabman, 1977). Playing a violent video game can also influence a person's internal state through the affective route by increasing feelings of anger, and through the arousal route by temporarily increasing heart rate (Anderson & Bushman, 2001). In sum, the General Aggression Model accounts for the wide variety of effects seen in the media violence literature, including both short-term and long-terms effects on aggressive thoughts, feelings, and behaviors, on emotional desensitization to violence and subsequent declines in prosocial behavior, and on changes in the social environment that occur as the developing child becomes more habitually aggressive.

It is interesting that the recent report on youth violence by the U.S. Surgeon General (U.S. Department of Health and Human Services, 2001) included exposure to television violence as a significant risk factor, but did not include exposure to violent video games in its risk factors list. There were a number of strange events surrounding the media violence portion of that report, some of which are briefly described in Anderson et al. (2003). Regardless of the political and other internal events that helped shape the final report, it is clear that one reason for the lack of a more specific statement regarding violent video game effects was the relatively small research literature on video games, especially the lack of longitudinal studies. The General Aggression Model, of course, predicts that repeated exposure to violent video games will indeed lead to increases in aggression. Other gaps in the video game literature include the potential of cartoonish violent video games to increase aggression, and the relative paucity of research linking video game violence exposure to real world aggression among the high school age population. The General Aggression Model predicts significant violent video game effects on aggression in both of these additional contexts.

PART II

NEW STUDIES

In Part II we present three new studies. These studies were designed to address knowledge gaps in the video game research literature described in the prior chapter. Chapter 4 presents Study 1, which examined the effects of exposure to the mildest form of violent video games (cartoonish children's games) on short-term aggressive behavior by children and college students. Chapter 5 presents Study 2, which examined the correlations between measures of video game violence exposure and aggressive behaviors among high school students, and included several important control variables. Chapter 6 presents Study 3, which examined the longitudinal effects of exposure to violent video games on aggression and prosocial behavior among elementary school children. All three studies examined additional risk factors and potential moderating variables as well, as suggested by the General Aggression Model, developmental models, and the risk and resilience approach. Chapter 7 further illustrates the effects of violent video games based on data from each of the three new studies.

Considerable statistical and methodological experience is needed to understand some of the detailed presentations of the results of these three new studies. However, because we hope that this book will be of interest to others with less statistical expertise or interest, we have also provided brief non-statistical summaries of the results in boxes in Chapters 4, 5, and 6.

For those without statistical expertise who nonetheless want to slog through the detailed results:

1. F values and t values are statistical tests.
2. p values give the statistical significance of the tests. When p is < 0.05, the result is statistically significant.
3. r values describe the association between two variables. They can range from -1 (a perfect negative correlation) through 0.0 (the variables are unrelated) to $+1.0$ (a perfect positive correlation).

4

Study 1: Experimental Study of Violent Video Games With Elementary School and College Students

Study 1 was designed to examine four main questions. First, can violent children's video games increase aggression (relative to a nonviolent children's video game) in a short-term experimental context? Second, would such a violent video game effect occur primarily for children or would it also occur for college students? Third, would T-rated violent video games (those rated "T" for teens and older) produce a bigger increase in aggression than the violent children's games? Fourth, would the short-term effects of playing a violent video game be moderated by sex, prior exposure to violent media, availability of video games in one's bedroom, preference for violent video games, and parental involvement in media usage? (For a brief description of the current industry-based ratings system and ratings of the games used in Study 1, see Appendix 2.)

Inclusion of a trait measure of violence allowed examination of several additional supplementary questions. First, does prior media violence exposure predict violence level? Second, how strong is this effect for new media (video games) versus old media (TV, film)? Third, does parental involvement moderate this effect?

Methods

Participants

Participants included 9- to 12-year-olds and 17- to 29-year-olds. Younger participants were recruited through ads placed in local newspapers and on university Web pages. Older participants were recruited from the psychology subject pool at a large Midwestern university. There were 161 younger participants (82 male, 79 female) and 354 older participants (178 male, 176 female). One participant switched video games in midstudy and was subsequently dropped from the experimental analyses. Each participant completed the study individually. College student participants were given course credit; all others were paid $20 for their participation.

Experimental Materials and Measures

Video Games

Five video games were used in this study: one nonviolent children's game (*Oh No! More Lemmings!*, $n = 163$, 92 old, 71 young); two violent children's games (*Captain Bumper*, $n = 110$, 64 old, 46 young; and *Otto Matic*, $n = 107$, 63 old, 44 young); and two violent games rated T, for 13 years and above (*Future Cop*, $n = 67$ old only; and *Street Fighter*, $n = 65$ old only). For ethical reasons the T-rated games were played only by the older participants. Because the nonviolent children's game condition was the comparison group for all of the children's and T-rated violent game conditions, there were more participants in this group to increase the power of specific comparisons. All video games were played on Macintosh iBook laptop computers for 20 minutes. Participants rated the games on several dimensions, including how action packed, entertaining, exciting, frustrating, fun, boring, and violent the games were.

Aggressive Behavior

The competitive reaction time task used in this study was a modification of the same basic computer program used by Bushman (1995), Anderson and Dill (2000), and Anderson, Anderson, Dorr, DeNeve, and Flanagan, (2000). It is based on the Taylor Competitive Reaction Time task, a widely used and well-validated laboratory measure of aggressive behavior (for summaries of validity tests and discussions, see Anderson & Bushman, 1997; Anderson, Lindsay, & Bushman, 1999; Bushman & Anderson, 1998; Bernstein, Richardson, & Hammock, 1987; Carlson et al., 1989; Giancola & Chermack, 1998). In this task, the participant's goal is to click the mouse (or track pad) button sooner than his or her opponent after receiving auditory or visual cues. When participants lose, they hear a punishing noise blast at an intensity supposedly set by their opponent (but actually set by the computer because there is no real opponent). This technique has been externally validated, meaning that people who are higher in aggression in the "real world" also provide higher noise blasts in the laboratory, and that laboratory findings based on this technique usually replicate when conceptually analogous studies are done in real-world contexts. It also has high internal validity, established by the fact that variables that theoretically should influence performance on it (e.g., provocation) do have such an influence, and that performance on this task corresponds well with other laboratory measures of aggressive behavior.

Participants completed 25 competitive reaction time trials, winning 13 and losing 12; the apparently random pattern of wins and losses was the same for each participant. Each trial began with the participant setting a noise intensity level they desired to send to their opponent by clicking on a scale that ranged from 0 to 10. After each trial, participants were shown on their computer screen the noise levels ostensibly set by their opponent. The pattern of noise intensities was designed to appear random. Noise intensity at Level 0 was at 0 decibels, 1 corresponded to 55 decibels, and the decibel level increased by 5 for each of the subsequent setting levels to a maximum of 100 decibels at Level 10. Aggressive behavior was operationally defined as the number of high-intensity noise blasts (settings of 8, 9, or 10) the participant chose to deliver to his or her opponent (Anderson & Murphy, 2003; Bartholow & Anderson, 2002; Bartholow, Anderson, Carnagey, & Benjamin, 2005; Giancola, 2003).

Post-Experimental Questionnaire

Experimental Game Ratings

Participants rated the game that they had been randomly assigned to play on seven dimensions. They did so by indicating their agreement with statements that the game was action packed, entertaining, exciting, frustrating, fun, boring, and violent. The scale was verbally anchored at −3 (*strongly disagree*), 0 (*neutral*), and 3 (*strongly agree*) (Anderson & Dill, 2000). Five of the items were combined into a single "entertainment" scale; these were the items on how action packed, entertaining, exciting, fun, and boring (reverse coded) the game was. Coefficient alpha for this scale was 0.88.

Violent Behavior History

The questionnaire included a nine-item violent behavior (VB) subscale from the Delinquency Scale used in a series of studies collectively called the National Youth Survey (e.g., Elliot, Huizinga, & Ageton, 1985; see also Anderson & Dill, 2000). The items ask participants to estimate how many times in the past year they have done each of the nine types of aggressive or violent behaviors, such as "attacked someone with the idea of seriously hurting him or her" and "used force (or threatened to use force) to get money or things from a teacher or other adult at school." One of the items was dropped, in part because of its low item-total correlation (0.05) and in part because of its potential ambiguity ["thrown objects (such as rocks, snowballs, or bottles) at cars or people?"] as an indicator of aggression, especially for children (i.e., snowball fights). Item scores were standardized and averaged. Coefficient alpha was 0.61, somewhat lower than in our previous usage (Anderson & Dill, 2000), perhaps because of the open-ended response format used in the present study. In addition, the violent behavior scores were extremely skewed, so a log transformation was used (Tukey, 1977).

Adult Involvement

The adult involvement in media scale (AIM) was included as an assessment of how involved adults are in the media habits of children (Buchanan, Gentile, Nelson, Walsh, & Hensel, 2002; Gentile, Linder, & Walsh, 2003; Gentile et al., 2004; Gentile & Walsh, 2002). The version used here comprised four questions: "How often does an adult watch TV or movies with you? How often does an adult talk to you about the TV or movies you watch? How often does an adult play video games with you? How often does an adult talk to you about the video games you play?" Response options were *never* (coded as a 1), *rarely* (2), *sometimes* (3), *often* (4), and *always* (coded as a 5). Coefficient alpha for the adult involvement in media scale was 0.71.

General Media Use Habits

Additional questions assessed general media habits (Buchanan et al., 2002; Gentile et al., 2003; Gentile et al., 2004; Gentile & Walsh, 2002). These questions focused on (a) specific media content ("How often do you watch MTV? How often do you watch wrestling on TV?"); (b) media location habits ("Do you have a TV in your bedroom? Do you play video games in your bedroom?"); and (c) media preferences ("How much violence do you like to have in video games? How much violence do you like to have in TV shows, or movies?"). The frequency and violence preference questions used the same 1–5 and 1–4 response options, respectively, as the media violence exposure items described in the next section. The violence preference items yielded a coefficient alpha of 0.72.

Next, a series of questions assessed how much time participants spent playing video games and watching TV and films (Buchanan et al., 2002; Gentile et al., 2003; Gentile et al., 2004; Gentile & Walsh, 2002). These questions asked participants to report how many hours they spent watching TV, seeing movies, and playing video games during very specific segments of the week ("when you wake up until lunch, between lunch and dinner, between dinner and bedtime") for typical school days and weekend days. The total number of hours was summed separately for video games, television, and movies, thereby providing a total amount of exposure for each.

Media Violence Exposure

A nine-item media violence exposure scale was created, based on the video game violence questionnaire used by Anderson & Dill (2000). In that earlier work the questionnaire was limited to the participants' exposure to video games; in this study questions were added to assess exposure to television and movies. Participants were asked to name their three favorite video games, TV shows, and movies. After naming these, participants rated how often they played or watched each game, show, or movie; response options were *almost never* (coded as a 1), *a couple of times a month* (2), *about once a week* (3), *about 2–3 times a week* (4), and *almost everyday* (coded as a 5). Next, participants rated how violent each game, show, or movie was; response options were *not at all violent* (coded as a 1), *a little violent* (2), *pretty violent* (3), and *very violent* (coded as a 4). For each of the nine specific media products (i.e., the three favorite video games, television shows, and movies) a violence exposure score was calculated by multiplying the frequency rating, the violence rating, and the total weekly time spent on that media type. The resulting nine scores composed the media violence exposure scale (MVE) for this study, and yielded a coefficient alpha of 0.90.

Procedure

Participants were run individually in 1-hour sessions. Upon completion of consent procedures, each participant was told that the researchers were interested in how playing different types of video games affected people's reaction times. Participants were read a set of standardized instructions concerning the competitive reaction time task and allowed to practice setting and hearing noise intensities before playing the assigned video game. Next, participants played their assigned video game with the experimenter present for about 5 minutes. Once each participant seemed capable of playing the game, the experimenter left him or her alone for 20 minutes of uninterrupted playing. After 20 minutes, the experimenter stopped the video game and reminded the participant that the goal of the reaction time task was to have the fastest reaction time; the experimenter then started the competitive computer reaction time task on the computer. Next, participants completed the postexperimental questionnaire and were debriefed.

STUDY 1 IN A NUTSHELL

Who Did What?

We tested 161 9- to 12-year-olds and 354 college students. Each participant was randomly assigned to play either a violent or a nonviolent video
game. In this context, violence is defined as intentional harm to a video
game character who is motivated to avoid that harm, and is not an indi-
cation of how graphic or gory the violence is. There was one children's
nonviolent game, two children's violent games with happy music and cartoonish game characters, and two violent games aimed at teens (T-rated).
The participants subsequently played another computer game in which
they set punishment levels (noxious noise blasts) to be delivered to another person participating in the study (this is a measure of aggressive behavior). Actually, there was no other person receiving the punishments.

We also gathered information about each participant's recent history
of violent behavior; habitual video game, television, and movie habits;
and several other control variables.

What Did We Expect?

We expected that participants who played one of the violent video
games (either child or teen focused) would choose to punish their opponents with higher noise blasts than those who played the nonviolent
video games. It was also possible that participants could deliver lower
noise blasts after playing the violent game (which would be evidence for
catharsis).

Furthermore, we expected that habitual exposure to violent media
would be positively associated with higher levels of violent behavior.

What Did We Actually Find?

We found that participants who played the violent video games pun-
ished their opponents with significantly more high-noise blasts than
those who played the nonviolent video games.

We also found that habitual exposure to violent media was positively
associated with higher levels of recent violent behavior. In addition, we
found that the newer interactive form of media violence (violent video
games) was more strongly related to violent behavior than was exposure
to noninteractive media violence (television, movies).

What Surprised Us?

We were somewhat surprised to find that even cartoonish children's violent games seemed to have the same short-term effect as the more
graphic T-rated (teen) violent games. People tend to believe that T-rated
games are *more* violent than E-rated (everyone) or other children's
games, but what seems to matter is whether the game includes aggres-

(*continued*)

sive content, not how realistic or graphic the violence is. If one counts the number of aggressive acts (intentional harm) within the games, they are about the same in both the children's and the teen violent games, even though the aggression is shown as much lighter and jollier in the children's games. Basically, it seems as though just practicing being aggressive led to higher aggression after playing, even if the game violence was not at all graphic, gory, or realistic.

We were also somewhat surprised that there was no apparent difference between the children and the college students. Many people have assumed that children are more vulnerable to media violence effects, but it seems that the college students were just as affected.

What Gives Us Hope?

Based on other surveys the participants completed, we found that what happens at home also seems to matter. Children whose parents are more involved in their media (e.g., setting limits on amount and content of games played) gave lower noise blasts in the lab and were less aggressive in their day-to-day lives (e.g., getting in fights). Furthermore, if children consumed a lot of media violence at home (TV, movies, DVDs, video games), they gave higher noise blasts in the lab and were more aggressive in their day-to-day lives. Putting these together, it suggests that parents are in a powerful position to minimize any negative effects of violent video games by limiting the types of games children play and how much time they may play them.

Results

The design is a 2 (age: children vs. college students) × 2 (children's game type: nonviolent vs. violent) factorial with one additional group (T-violent games played by the older participants). Therefore contrast analyses were used to test specific effects. The first was a contrast comparing the average of the violent game conditions versus the nonviolent game conditions. Next, a series of three contrasts performed a standard 2 × 2 (age × violent vs. nonviolent children's game) analysis of variance (ANOVA), ignoring the T-violent game.

Effect sizes for categorical group differences are reported as d values, calculated by dividing the difference between the two relevant adjusted means by the pooled standard deviation. Effect sizes for continuous variables are reported as r values. Note that the r values for the unique effect of a predictor variable after other control variables have been accounted for are partial correlations.

Ratings of the Assigned Video Game

Entertainment Ratings

Overall, the violent games were rated as more entertaining than the non-violent game (on the composite measure), $F(1, 506) = 5.65, p < 0.05$. The 2×2 (age $\times$ children's game violence) analyses yielded significant main effects of age and children's game violence, Fs$(1, 506) = 39.93$ and 5.54, ps < 0.001 and $.05$, ds $= .67$ and $.23$, respectively. Neither the sex main effect nor the age $\times$ children's game violence interaction approached significance, Fs$(1, 506) = 0.00$ and 0.61. Table 4.1 contains the means.

Frustration Ratings

Overall, the violent and nonviolent games did not reliably differ in frustration, $F(1, 506) = 1.09, p > 0.2$. The 2×2 analysis yielded a significant main effect of children's game violence, $F(1, 506) = 3.87, p < 0.05$, $d = 0.24$. As can be seen in Table 4.1, the nonviolent game was rated as somewhat more frustrating than the children's violent games. Neither the age main effect nor the age $\times$ children's game violence interaction were significant, Fs$(1, 506) = 1.57$ and 2.78, ps > 0.09. The sex main effect was highly significant, $F(1, 506) = 25.31, p < 0.001, d = 0.50$. Males reported a higher level of frustration $(M = 0.46)$ than females $(M = -0.31)$.

Violence Ratings

Overall, the violent games were rated as much more violent than the nonviolent game, $F(1, 506) = 172.06, p < 0.001, d = 1.17$. In addition, the sex main effect was significant, $F(1, 506) = 10.32, p < 0.005, d = 0.29)$. Males rated the games as less violent than females, Ms $= -1.22$ and -0.78, respectively. The 2×2 analysis of children's games yielded a significant

TABLE 4.1   Mean ratings of the assigned video games by age.

Experimental Game Condition	Participant Age Group	Entertainment Composite	Frustration	Violence
Children's—Violent	Old	−.23	−.45	−.85
Children's—Violent	Young	.48	.09	−1.04
Children's—Nonviolent	Old	−.39	.22	−2.12
Children's—Nonviolent	Young	.17	.14	−2.21
Teen—Violent	Old	.07	.38	1.24

Notes: Age Group: Old ranged from 17–29; Young ranged from 9–12. All ratings were on Likert-type scales that ranged from −3 (strongly disagree) to +3 (strongly agree). The entertainment composite is the average of five rating dimensions: action packed, entertaining, exciting, fun, and boring (reverse coded).

main effect of game violence, $F(1, 506) = 55.73$, $p < 0.001$, $d = 0.79$. The children's violent games were rated as more violent than the nonviolent game. Neither the age main effect nor the age × children's game violence interaction approached significance, $Fs < 1$. The means, displayed in Table 4.1, reveal two interesting features. First, the children's games were rated below the violence scale midpoint. Second, only the T-violent games were rated as having any appreciable level of violence.

Summary

Two interesting points emerged from the ratings of the experimental games. First, the fact that reliable differences emerged among game types on entertainment and frustration suggests that it might be useful to use these two dimensions as covariates in some analyses of the short-term aggressive behavior data, *if* either dimension correlates significantly with the aggression measure. Second, the fact that participants rated the children's violent games as less violent than the T-violent games confirms our suspicions that features other than amount or frequency of harm contribute significantly to people's perceptions of violent content. Both of the children's violent games consist of almost continuous violent attacks on the enemies, just as in the two T-violent games. However, the children's violent games are accompanied by happy music and highly cartoonish nonhuman targets. If such features protect the game player from the aggression-enhancing potential of the violent actions, then we should find no increase in aggression (relative to the nonviolent game) in the violent children's game conditions, and a heightened level of aggression only in the T-violent condition. However, if the violent actions somehow activate aggressive scripts or thought patterns, then even the children's violent games should increase aggression.

Short-Term Aggression in the Lab

The primary dependent measure was the number of trials in the reaction time competition (out of 25) on which the participant set the noise level at 8 or higher. This high-intensity noise blasts (HI) measure was quite skewed and there was a tendency for group standard deviations to be positively related to group means, so a square root transformation was used (Tukey, 1977). Adjusted means were converted back to the original scale (i.e., 0–25 high-intensity attempts) for reporting purposes.

Game Ratings

Preliminary analyses revealed that neither of the two control dimensions (the entertainment composite and frustration of the game played) correlated reliably with the laboratory aggression measure (rs = 0.06 and 0.07, ps > 0.10). Therefore, it was unnecessary (and perhaps inappropriate) to use them as covariates in analyses of video game effects on aggression.[1]

Main Analyses

The results of the main analyses of high-intensity noise blasts were very clear. There were no hints of main or interaction effects involving age, or of interaction effects involving sex, ps > 0.2. However, males behaved more aggressively than females, Ms = 8.26 and 3.34, $F(1, 506)$ = 76.76, $p < 0.001$, $d = 0.78$.

Of considerably more interest are the effects of game violence. Figure 4.1 displays the adjusted means. As expected, participants who played one of the violent games delivered more high-intensity noise blasts than those who played the nonviolent game, $F(1, 506)$ = 7.49, $p < 0.01$. The 2 × 2 ANOVA (excluding the T-violent condition) yielded a significant main effect of video game violence, $F(1, 506)$ = 9.48, $p < 0.005$, $d = 0.32$. As can be seen in Figure 4.1, participants in the children's violent game conditions delivered significantly more high-intensity noise blasts than did those in the nonviolent game conditions, over 40% more in both age groups.

Additional contrasts revealed that the children's violent games significantly increased aggression by the younger and the older participants separately, relative to the nonviolent game, $Fs(1, 506)$ = 4.78 and 4.76, $ps < 0.03$. Furthermore, older participants assigned to play any of the violent games (children's or T-rated) delivered significantly more high-intensity blasts than their nonviolent condition counterparts, $F(1, 506)$ = 4.14, $p < .05$.

The lack of an age × game interaction may come as a surprise to those who believe that children are much more vulnerable to media violence effects. It is important to keep four facts in mind. First, there is little experimental evidence of such an age-based vulnerability to short-term media violence effects on aggression. Second, the best current evidence supporting the childhood vulnerability hypothesis comes from longitudinal studies. Third, the General Aggression Model (and its developmental aspects) predicts that childhood vulnerability effects are most likely to appear in long-term, repeated exposure contexts, rather than in short-term contexts such as the present experiment. Fourth, there is a hint in the present

---

[1] Adding these variables to the statistical model had no appreciable impact on the results. All of the significant effects of the video game manipulation reported in the following section remained significant with one exception: the overall effect of violent games (E- or T-rated) versus the nonviolent game for older participants became marginally significant, $p < 0.06$, when the composite entertainment factor was in the model.

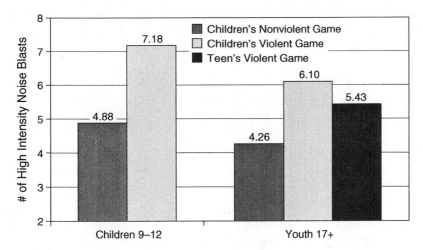

Figure 4.1 Aggression as a function of game type and age.

data that the children's violent video games had a slightly larger effect on the younger ($d = 0.35$) than on the older ($d = 0.30$) participants in this experiment.

The lack of a significant difference between the violent children's game condition and the "T" condition for the older participants may also come as a surprise, at least to those who place a lot of faith in the video game industry's rating system. But as noted earlier, the violent children's games involve almost continuous violent behavior, just as in the T-rated violent games selected for this experiment.

Individual Difference Effects on Laboratory Aggression

To further explore the high-intensity noise blasts findings, we conducted a series of analyses on several individual difference variables for participants who had played one of the children's games. Three questions were of primary interest. First, which (if any) of the individual difference variables significantly predict laboratory aggression, controlling for sex, age, and game condition.[2] Second, was the children's game violence effect still

---

[2] As noted earlier, from a theoretical perspective variables that normally should predict long-term aggressiveness (e.g., habitual media violence exposure) might not predict laboratory aggression in experimental studies, especially if the experimentally manipulated variables exert a powerful effect. That is, sometimes brief but powerful manipulations can override (temporarily) more chronic individual difference variables (see Anderson, 1983, for an example in the depression and motivation domain).

significant when the individual difference variables were statistically controlled? Third, which (if any) of the individual difference variables moderate the children's game violence effect?

Media Violence Exposure

Media violence exposure (the composite of television, film, and video game violence exposure) was positively related to the number of high-intensity noise blasts delivered, $r(381) = 0.17$, $p < 0.001$. However, when sex, age, and children's game violence condition were statistically controlled, the media violence exposure effect was reduced to nonsignificance, $p = 0.10$. The effect of children's game violence remained significant in this model, with higher aggression levels displayed by those who had just played a violent game, $F(1, 375) = 9.04$, $p < 0.005$, $d = 0.31$. Media violence exposure did not interact with children's game violence ($p > 0.5$), indicating that the children's game violence effect on short-term aggression was of essentially the same magnitude regardless of the participant's history of exposure to media violence.

Bedroom Media

Simply having a TV in one's bedroom was not significantly associated with higher levels of aggression in the lab, but playing video games in one's bedroom was linked to setting more high-intensity noises, $r(380) = 0.19$, $p < 0.001$. The bedroom gaming effect remained significant when sex, age, and game condition were statistically controlled, $F(1, 373) = 4.29$, $p < 0.05$. The effect of children's game violence remained significant in this model, $F(1, 373) = 9.09$, $p < 0.005$, $d = 0.32$. Bedroom gaming did not interact with children's game violence ($p > 0.5$), indicating that the children's game violence effect was of essentially the same magnitude regardless of whether the participant played video games in the bedroom.

Violence Preferences

Violence preference was positively correlated with high-intensity noise blasts, $r(374) = 0.25$, $p < 0.001$. The violence preference effect remained significant when sex, age, and game condition were statistically controlled, $F(1, 367) = 8.06$, $p < 0.005$. The effect of children's game violence remained significant in this model, $F(1, 367) = 8.97$, $p < 0.005$, $d = 0.32$. Violence preference did not interact with children's game violence ($p > 0.5$), indicating that the children's game violence effect was of essentially the same magnitude regardless of the participant's preference for violent media.

Adult Involvement

The zero-order correlation between the adult involvement in media scale and high-intensity noise blasts was not significant, but the adult involvement in media scale was significantly negatively associated with high-intensity noise blasts once sex, age, and game condition were statistically controlled, $F(1, 372) = 5.94$, $p < 0.02$. The negative association means that participants whose parents were more involved in their media use gave fewer high-intensity noise blasts. More interesting was the adult involvement in media × children's game violence interaction, $F(1, 372) = 5.47$, $p < 0.02$, which is displayed in Figure 4.2. Additional analyses revealed that adult involvement in media was negatively related to high-intensity noise blasts in the children's violent game conditions, $b = -0.35$, $t(213) = 3.62$, $p < 0.001$, but was unrelated to high-intensity noise blasts in the nonviolent game conditions, $b = -0.01$, $t(157) = 0.11$. This indicates that adult involvement might considerably reduce the short-term effects of playing violent video games. However, the adult involvement in media variable was measured, not manipulated, so interpretive caution is warranted.

The main effect of children's game violence remained significant in the model containing the adult involvement in media × children's game violence interaction, $F(1, 372) = 9.59$, $p < 0.005$, $d = 0.30$. Additional interaction terms involving adult involvement in media were examined; none was significant.

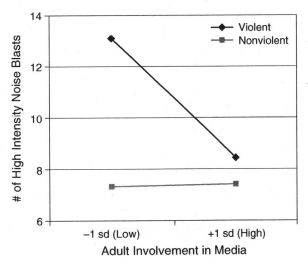

Figure 4.2 Number of high-intensity blasts as a function of adult involvement and children's game type.

Media Violence Exposure and Violent Behavior

Recall that violent behavior history was assessed after the main experimental manipulations and measurements had taken place to reduce the possibility of participants getting suspicious about the main purpose of the study. Therefore, the regression analyses in this section included a categorical variable indicating the video game condition of the participant to control for possible experimental condition effects on these individual difference measures. Sex and age were also included as statistical controls. Because violent behavior history was so highly skewed, a log transformation was used in all data analyses.

Main Regression Results

Media violence exposure was positively associated with violent behavior, $r = 0.20$, $p < 0.001$. The media violence exposure effect remained significant even after controlling for sex, age, and game condition, $F(1, 506) = 14.89$, $p < .0001$, $r = 0.17$. Additional tests were conducted to examine the possibility that media violence exposure might interact with age or sex. Neither two-way interaction was significant, $ps > 0.10$.

Adult Involvement as a Moderator

We conducted additional analyses on the children's data to see whether adult involvement interacted with media violence exposure as a moderator. We first examined the main effects of media violence exposure, game condition, sex, and adult involvement in media on violent behavior. Media violence exposure contributed a significant unique increment to the prediction of violent behavior. Higher media violence exposure scores were associated with higher levels of aggression, $F(1, 155) = 8.78$, $p < 0.005$, $r = 0.23$. The main effect of game condition was also significant, $F(1, 155) = 4.30$, $p < 0.05$. Those who had just played one of the violent children's games reported slightly lower levels of prior violent behavior. Whether this is the result of children randomly assigned to the nonviolent game truly having a slightly more violent history than those assigned to a violent children's game, or results from some type of biased reporting of past behavior created by just playing a violent or nonviolent game, cannot be determined. In either case, this finding further justifies using game condition as a control variable in analyses of these postexperimental scales.

We next added the interaction term for media violence exposure and adult involvement in media, which proved significant, $F(1, 154) = 10.36$, $p < 0.005$. To further examine this interaction, we used regression procedures to test the effect of media violence exposure on violent behavior at one standard deviation above the adult involvement in media mean (i.e., high adult involvement) and one standard deviation below the mean (i.e., low adult involvement). The results were quite clear. For children whose parents were essentially uninvolved in their media usage, media violence exposure was positively related to reports of violent behavior, $F(1, 154) = 17.07$, $p < 0.0001$. However, the media violence exposure link to violent behavior was nonsignificant for children whose parents were highly involved, $F < 1$. These results are very similar to the adult involvement interaction found with the experimental effects of children's game violence on laboratory aggression, and further suggest that adult involvement with children's media exposure might reduce the negative impact of media violence. Experimental and longitudinal studies on adult involvement as a possible protective factor are needed to test this implication.

Old Versus New Violent Media

To compare the effects of new interactive violent media (i.e., video games) with older forms of media violence (i.e., television and movies), two subscales were created from the nine-item media violence exposure scale. The three-item video game violence exposure scale yielded an alpha of 0.90. The six-item television and movie violence exposure scale yielded an alpha of 0.91. Exposure to both new and old forms of media violence correlated significantly with violent behavior, $rs = 0.20$ and 0.16 respectively, $ps < 0.001$.

We ran three additional regression models, each with sex, age, and game condition as control variables. The first also included the measure of new violent media exposure; the only significant effect was that video game violence was positively associated with violent behavior, $F(1, 506) = 14.34$, $p < 0.0002$, $b = 0.0429$, $r = 0.17$. The second model included the measure of old violent media exposure instead of video game violence; the only significant effect was that television and movie violence was positively associated with violent behavior, $F(1, 506) = 9.12$, $p < 0.003$, $b = 0.0009$, $r = 0.13$. The third included both measures of violent media exposure. Video game violence exposure yielded a significant unique positive association with violent behavior even after controlling for sex, age, game condition, and older violent media exposure, $[F(1, 505) = 6.67, p < 0.02, b = 0.0335, r = 0.11]$; the television and movie violence exposure effect became nonsignificant, $F(1, 505) = 1.53$, $p > 0.20$, $b = 0.0004$, $r = 0.06$. In other words, video game violence exposure was a stronger predictor of violent behavior than was television and movie violence exposure.

Finally, we added two-way interaction terms to the video game violence and television and movie violence models to see whether either of the media violence exposure measures interacted with age or with sex in the prediction of violent behavior. None of the interactions of media violence by age or media violence by sex were significant, $ps > 0.10$.

Summary of Media Violence and Violent Behavior Results

Though not the main focus of this study, these results yielded additional support for the broad hypothesis that repeated exposure to violent media can lead to increases in violent behavior. In addition, adult involvement in children's media consumption appeared to mitigate to some extent the deleterious effect of high exposure to violent media. Finally, the newer interactive form of violent media (video games) had a larger impact on violent behavior than the older form (television and movies). As video games become more pervasive, more violent, more realistic, and consume a larger portion of entertainment time, the relative impact of violent video games may begin to consistently outstrip the negative impact of violent television and films.

Discussion

Study 1 was designed to examine four main and three supplementary questions. The most important result was the finding that brief exposure to children's games with violent content can cause an increase in aggression in a short-term context. The happy music, cute cartoonish characters, and nonhuman enemies characteristic of children's violent games do not eradicate the aggression-inducing potential of these games. A second important result was that this effect occurred in both the child and the college student population. Indeed, the effect appeared only slightly larger for the younger than for the older sample. The third finding was that the T-rated violent games did not produce a larger increase in short-term aggression than the violent children's games. Indeed, the T-violent games yielded a slightly (and nonsignificantly) lower level of aggression than the children's violent games. The fourth main question concerned potential moderator effects. As noted earlier, age did not change the children's game violence effect. Neither did sex, habitual prior exposure to violent media, availability of video games in one's bedroom, or preference for violent video games. However, high parental involvement in media usage appeared to provide some protection against the children's game violence effect in this short-term context. In brief, the data revealed that the children's game violence effect on short-term aggression occurred for males and females, for children and college students, for those with much and those with little previous exposure to violent media, for those with and without video games in the bedroom, and those with high or low preference for violent media. Finally, several of these factors proved to be risk factors for aggression in this short-term context. Being male, having habitual prior exposure to media violence, having video games in the bedroom, and preferring violent media all led to significantly higher levels of aggression on the competitive reaction time task.

The supplementary analyses on the trait measure of violent behavior also yielded several important findings. A history of prior media violence exposure was associated with violent behavior. This effect was stronger for new media (video games) than old media. And parental involvement moderated the media violence exposure effect to some extent.

In sum, Study 1 replicated many prior findings in this area as well as answered some previously untested questions. Perhaps the most important new finding was that even children's video games can increase aggression of children and college students if the games contain a lot violent action. That is, the cartoonish images, happy music, and lack of blood (or realism) do not eliminate the short-term effects of violent video games on aggression.

Study 2 was designed to fill another gap in the existing research literature. Specifically, it was designed to examine a number of potential violent video game effects in a high school population.

5

Study 2: Correlational Study With High School Students

Study 2 was a cross-section correlational study of media habits, aggression-related individual difference variables, and aggressive behaviors on an adolescent population. As noted earlier, there is very little research on the effects of habitual video game violence exposure with this population. One of the individual difference variables was a newly developed scale designed to measure aggressive normative beliefs. The primary goals of this study were (a) to test the hypothesis that habitual exposure to violent video games is associated with higher levels of physical aggression and violence, (b) to examine the strength of that association by statistically controlling for several key competing predictor variables, and (c) to test the General Aggression Model–based hypothesis that habitual exposure to violent video games is associated with certain types of attitudes toward violence and with aggressive normative beliefs. Specifically, we expected that video game violence would correlate most strongly with attitudes toward war, and least with attitudes toward corporal punishment of children. Violent video games often involve war themes, including re-creations of old, recent, and current wars; Special Forces, anti-terrorist actions, and hostage rescue; and futuristic fights against alien invaders or conquerors. Few games (if any) model and reward violence against children. We also expected video game violence to correlate positively with beliefs that aggression in normal family and social situations is relatively common. However, because most violent video games involve war-like contexts, we did not expect this correlation to be large.

Two less central hypotheses were also addressed. First, we included a recently developed measure of trait forgiveness because of its theoretical relation to aggression. Specifically, we hypothesized that trait forgivingness would be negatively correlated with aggression. Second, we also examined the hypothesis that high levels of screen time (television, movies, and video games) would be associated with poorer school performance.

Methods

Participants

One hundred eighty-nine students, 76 males and 113 females, were recruited from two small Iowa high schools and received $10 for their participation. The age distribution was as follows: 15 years, 13%; 16 years, 35%; 17 years, 34%; 18 years, 16%. There was one 14-year-old and one 19-year-old. Seven participants did not report their age. Ninety-eight percent of the sample was Caucasian, reflecting the racial composition of rural Iowa.

Materials

Participants completed a questionnaire packet that included personality and behavioral measures related to media and aggression. Specifically, participants completed measures of aggression norms and attitudes, forgiveness, aggressiveness, violence, exposure to video games, and aggressive cognitions. We also asked participants for their grade point average (GPA). Internal reliabilities (coefficient alpha) for multiple item scales were sufficiently large; the lowest was 0.74 for the forgivingness scale.

Attitudes Toward Violence

The *revised attitudes toward violence scale* (RATVS; Anderson, Benjamin, Wood, & Bonacci, 2006) taps attitudes toward four types of aggression: penal code violence (PCV, e.g., "A law enforcement officer should shoot citizens if they are murder suspects"), violence in war (WAR, e.g., "War is often necessary"), corporal punishment of children (CPC, e.g., "An adult should choke a child for breaking the law"), and violence between intimates (INT, e.g., "It is all right for a partner to slap the other's face if challenged"). The four subscales emerged from latent variable analyses, and are somewhat intercorrelated. The revised attitudes toward violence scale successfully predicts violent behavior, physical aggression, and verbal aggression (Anderson et al., 2006). The alpha coefficients from the present sample for the penal code, war, corporal punishment, and intimate violence subscales were 0.78, 0.83, 0.86, and 0.87, respectively. The coefficient alpha for the revised attitudes toward violence scale as a whole was 0.92.

Aggressive Behavior, Hostility, and Anger

The Buss Perry Aggression Questionnaire (AQ; Buss & Perry, 1992) consists of four subscales assessing physical and verbal aggression (PA, VA, respectively), the emotional component anger, and hostility. Agreement with statements such as, "I get into fights a little more than the average person," and "I can't help getting into arguments when people disagree with me," indicate higher physical and verbal aggression, respectively. Agreement with statements such as, "I have trouble controlling my temper," and "I wonder why I sometimes feel so bitter about things," indicate higher anger and hostility, respectively. The alpha coefficients for the physical, verbal, anger, and hostility subscales were 0.86, 0.78, 0.83, and 0.76, respectively. Coefficient alpha for the complete aggression questionnaire was 0.92.

Trait Forgivingness

The *trait forgivingness scale* (TFS) measures individuals' tendency to forgive interpersonal transgressions over time and across situations (Berry, Worthington, O'Connor, Parrott, Wade, 2005). Individuals who score high on the forgivingness scale agree with statements such as, "I can forgive a friend for almost anything," and "I try to forgive others even when they do not feel guilty for what they did." Coefficient alpha for the forgivingness scale was 0.74.

Normative Aggressive Beliefs

A new nine-item scale was designed to assess participants' beliefs about the normativeness of certain types of aggressive behavior. This *normative aggression beliefs* (NAB) scale assesses beliefs about how often aggressive behaviors occur. Individuals who score high on the normative aggression beliefs scale believe that events such as spanking, verbal fights, and physical fights occur more often than do individuals who score low. See Table 5.1 for a complete list of items. The coefficient alpha for the normative aggression beliefs scale was 0.83. It is important to note that this new measure differs conceptually from Krahé and Möller's (2004) similarly named measure. Their measure was designed to assess the extent to which individuals *condone* aggression, whereas our new measure assesses the extent to which individuals believe that aggressive acts are common (or uncommon).

TABLE 5.1   Items from the Normative Aggression Beliefs scale

1. What percentage of parents in the UnitedStates spank their children?
2. What percentage of married couples have a physical fight (involving hitting, slapping, or other physical fighting behaviors) in a given year?
3. What percentage of dating couples have a physical fight (involving hitting, slapping, or other physical fighting behaviors) in a given 6-month period?
4. What percentage of college men get into a physical fight with another person (any person) at least once a year?
5. What percentage of college women get into a physical fight with another person (any person) at least once a year?
6. What percentage of married couples have a verbal fight (involving yelling, screaming, or other verbal fighting behaviors) in a given year?
7. What percentage of dating couples have a verbal fight (involving yelling, screaming, or other verbal fighting behaviors) in a given 6-month period?
8. What percentage of college men get into a verbal fight with another person (any person) at least once a year?
9. What percentage of college women get into a verbal fight with another person (any person) at least once a year?

Violent behavior

Self-reported violent behavior was again assessed using 10 items from the National Youth Survey. This time, however, response options (frequency in the last year) were constrained rather than open ended: 0, 1–3, 4–6, 7–9, 10–12, 13–15, 16–18, 19–21, 22–24, 25–27, more than 27. Responses were coded with the midvalue of the range indicated, except the highest category, which was coded as 29. As in Study 1, items were standardized, averaged, and then subjected to a log transformation to reduce the skewness of the distribution. The coefficient alpha for violent behavior history was 0.85. Unlike in Study 1, the item concerning throwing objects (such as rocks, snowballs, or bottles) at cars or people correlated well with the other violent behavior items. Furthermore, supplemental analyses revealed that deleting this item did not significantly change the violent behavior scale correlation with video game violence exposure. Finally, the item is less ambiguous in meaning for high school students than for elementary students, in large part because the throwing of snowballs is less frequently a play activity. Therefore, the item was retained in this study.

Media Exposure

Individuals' exposure to violent video games was measured using the *video game violence scale* (Anderson & Dill, 2000). On this scale individuals list up to five favorite video games, report how often they have played each in recent months, and rate the violence of each game. For each game the frequency of play is multiplied by the rated violence. In the present study participants also indicated how often they played each game in seventh and eighth grade. Preliminary analyses found very similar results from both periods, so video game violence scores from recent months and from seventh and eighth grades were averaged to produce an overall video game violence score for each participant.

We also created a total screen time (TST) measure by asking participants to indicate, "How many hours per week (on average) do you spend playing video and computer games? watching television? watching movies at theaters or at home on videotape or cable TV?" The total from these three items constituted the measure of total screen time. The purpose of this measure was to see whether sheer volume of time spent on such leisure activities was more (or less) important than video game violence exposure in predicting various outcomes. Based on prior research (e.g., Anderson & Dill, 2000) we expected video game violence to be a more important predictor of physical aggression and violence but total screen time to be a better predictor of grade point average.

Participants also indicated the percentage of their television and movie time that was spent watching materials that contain some violent content. Each of these two percentages were multiplied by their corresponding hours-per-week estimates to create television and movie violence exposure estimates.

Procedure

Data for this study were collected in high school classrooms. Participants were informed of the study and given parental consent forms by their teacher; only those who had parental approval were allowed to participate. At the start of each session, the researcher explained that the experimenters were interested in the opinions and activities of high school students. Participants completed the questionnaire packet and were given $10.

Results

In the first section, on zero order correlations, we highlight some specific patterns of correlations relevant to the General Aggression Model and to media habits. We then turn to destructive testing regression procedures to further test our three main hypotheses concerning video game violence effects on aggression, forgivingness effects on aggression, and screen time effects on grade point average.

STUDY 2 IN A NUTSHELL

Who Did What?

We gave surveys to 189 high school students. The surveys included measures of (1) violent TV, movie, and video game exposure, (2) attitudes toward violence, (3) personality trait hostility, (4) personality trait forgivingness, (5) beliefs about how normal violence is, and (6) their frequency of various verbally and physically aggressive behaviors.

What Did We Expect?

We expected that adolescents who play a greater number of violent video games would hold more pro-violent attitudes, have more hostile personalities, be less forgiving, believe violence to be more typical, and to behave more aggressively in their everyday lives. Again, the study was designed such that adolescents who played more violent video games could also be less aggressive (which would be evidence for catharsis).

What Did We Actually Find?

We found what we expected—adolescents who play a greater number of violent video games hold more pro-violent attitudes, have more hostile personalities, are less forgiving, believe violence to be more typical, and behave more aggressively in their everyday lives. However, because this study did not manipulate who plays violent or nonviolent games, it is possible that some other variable accounts for the findings. For example, males tend to be more aggressive in personality, attitudes, and behaviors, and also tend to play more violent video games. However, even after statistically controlling for sex, total screen time, aggressive beliefs and attitudes, we still found that playing violent video games was a significant predictor of heightened physically aggressive behavior and violent behavior.

What Surprised Us?

We were somewhat surprised to find that the relation between violent video game play was as strong as it is. That is, we expected that some other theoretically relevant variables (i.e., being a boy, having an aggressive personality, etc.) would account equally well for why some kids behave more aggressively; and although those all predict aggressive behavior, they don't tell the whole story—violent video game play still made an additional difference.

We were also somewhat surprised that there was no apparent difference in the video game violence effect between boys and girls or adolescents with already aggressive attitudes. Many people have assumed that boys who are already aggressive in outlook are more vulnerable to media

(continued)

STUDY 2 IN A NUTSHELL (*continued*)

violence effects, but it seems that all groups are equally affected. However, one variable—trait forgivingness—did yield different results, but only for the violent behavior measure. Adolescents who scored high on a measure of personality trait forgivingness appeared to be somewhat less affected by exposure to violent video games, at least on the violent behavior measures.

What Worries Us About These Results?

It appears that no one is truly "immune" from the effects of media violence exposure.

What Else Did We Find?

Screen time (TV and video game time combined) was a significant negative predictor of grades. That is, the more time adolescents spend in front of a screen, the worse their school performance. We also found evidence that the relation between violent video game exposure and both physical aggression and violent behavior may be stronger than the relation between violent TV and movie exposure and physical aggression and violent behavior.

Zero Order Correlations

Video Game Violence Effects

Violent video games always model and reward physical aggression, and sometimes model (but do not reward) verbal aggression. Thus, violent video games are likely to have a bigger impact on physical than verbal aggression. The video game violence correlations with the three aggression measures yielded this expected pattern. As shown in Table 5.2, video game violence was positively correlated with violent behavior ($r = 0.35$) and physical aggression ($r = 0.46$). It also correlated positively with verbal aggression, but at a somewhat lower level ($r = 0.25$). Total time spent on screen media (TV, movies, video games) also correlated significantly with all three aggression measures, $rs = 0.16$ to 0.29.

As noted earlier, because of the specific type of violence contained in most popular violent video games we expected that video game violence would correlate most strongly with attitudes toward war and least with attitudes toward corporal punishment of children. This is exactly what happened, with video game violence correlating most strongly with attitudes toward war ($r = 0.36$) and weakly with attitudes toward corporal punishment of children ($r = 0.12$).

We also expected a small positive correlation between video game violence and normative aggression beliefs. The obtained correlation ($r = 0.15$) met this expectation.

Predicting Grade Point Average

It is interesting to note that video game violence was not significantly correlated with grade point average, but total screen time was negatively correlated with grade point average ($r = -0.29$). High school students who spend more time consuming various types of screen media have lower grade point averages. This replicates the results that Anderson and Dill (2000) found with college student participants and that Gentile et al. (2004) found with adolescents. Grade point average was also negatively correlated with violence, physical aggression, and a variety of aggressive attitudes and beliefs.

Attitudes Toward and Beliefs About Violence

All four attitudes toward violence subscales correlated significantly with all three aggression measures with one exception, the correlation of attitude toward corporal punishment of children with violent behavior was nonsignificant. Physical aggression and violent behavior were best predicted by attitudes toward violence between intimates and war attitudes. Also, beliefs about the normativeness of aggression correlated positively and significantly with both violent behavior and physical aggression but were not significantly correlated with verbal aggression.

Positive Orientation to Violence

Closer inspection of Table 5.2 reveals that the four attitudes toward violence subscales along with the anger and hostility subscales tended to correlate with each other ($rs = 0.17$ to 0.63). We therefore created a global *positive orientation to violence scale* (POV) to reduce the overall number of predictor variables to be used in subsequent regression analyses. Coefficient alpha for this 54-item scale was 0.91. Positive orientation to violence was positively correlated with video game violence ($r = 0.34$), total screen time ($r = 0.32$), violent behavior ($r = 0.43$), physical aggression ($r = 0.66$), and verbal aggression ($r = 0.43$), all $ps < 0.001$. Positive orientation to violence was also negatively correlated with trait forgivingness ($r = -0.33$) and grade point average ($r = -0.37$), $ps < 0.001$. It was largely unrelated to normative beliefs about aggression ($r = 0.08$), which indicates that the normative aggression beliefs scale measures something different from the subscales composing the positive orientation to violence scale.

Of course, zero-order correlations do not always yield a complete picture. For example, the significant violent video game correlations with ag-

TABLE 5.2 Correlations of key variables, high school students (alpha coefficients are on the diagonal in italics)

Measure	Media Use		Aggressive Behavior			Trait			Attitudes Toward Violence				
	VGV	TST	VB	PA	VA	Anger	Host.	PCV	WAR	CPC	INT	NAB	TFS
VGV	.82												
TST	.25	na											
VB	.35	.16	.85										
PA	.46	.29	.56	.86									
VA	.25	.25	.33	.48	.78								
Anger	.23	.21	.41	.67	.61	.83							
Host.	.21	.21	.30	.44	.45	.63	.76						
PCV	.16	.15	.15	.32	.09	.18	.19	.78					
WAR	.36	.18	.28	.43	.18	.20	.21	.56	.83				
CPC	.12	.16	.10	.26	.16	.18	.17	.37	.34	.86			
INT	.20	.34	.45	.47	.22	.31	.18	.33	.36	.52	.87		
NAB	.15	.01	.17	.16	.06	.17	.13	.07	.00	-.05	.03	.83	
TFS	-.14	.00	-.32	-.39	-.41	-.39	-.39	-.15	-.12	-.09	-.22	-.14	.74
GPA	-.05	-.29	-.24	-.38	-.11	-.23	-.15	-.18	-.16	-.33	-.44	-.04	.11

ns range from 178-189. $p < .05$ if $r \geq .15$. VGV = video game violence; TST = total screen time; VB = violent behavior; PA = physical aggression; VA = verbal aggression; Anger = trait anger; Host. = trait hostility; PCV = attitudes toward penal code violence; WAR = attitudes toward violence in war; CPC = attitudes toward corporal punishment of children; INT = attitudes toward violence against intimates; NAB = normative aggression beliefs; TFS = trait forgivingness scale; GPA = grade point average.

gression might disappear if other competitor variables (such as sex, total screen time) are statistically controlled. Furthermore, still other variables (such as positive orientation to violence) might serve as mediators of the effects of habitual exposure to violent video games on violence and aggression. Regression analyses were conducted to further explore these questions.

Regression Analyses: Destructive Testing

Our first set of regression analyses used a destructive testing approach as described by Anderson and Anderson (1996) and used by Anderson and Dill (2000). This approach begins by examining whether a predicted relation between two target variables (e.g., video game violence, physical aggression) is statistically reliable. If it is, the strength of that relation is tested (or stressed) by systematically adding theoretically relevant covariates to the statistical model until the link between the two target variables is broken (i.e., becomes nonsignificant) or until one runs out of relevant covariates. It is assumed that adding covariates will eventually break the target link. One judges the validity of the original link not by whether it can be broken, but by how easy or difficult it is to break the link. If the link is easily broken by one or two theoretically relevant covariates that provide an alternative explanation, then confidence in the validity of that link should be relatively low. However, if inclusion of several theoretically relevant covariates fails to break the link, then confidence in the validity of the original relation between the two target variables should be high. In other words, the theoretical and empirical status of the covariates must be considered when evaluating the destructive testing results. A given covariate may be conceived of as a nuisance variable (e.g., sex of participant), a theoretical competitor variable (e.g., total screen time), or a potential mediating variable (e.g., attitudes toward violence). For example, if the media violence–aggression link is broken by adding the single theoretical competitor variable of "total screen time," the link (zero-order correlation) between media violence and aggressive behavior should not be seen as providing strong support for the media violence–aggression hypothesis. However, if the potential mediating variable "attitudes toward violence" breaks the link, this break should not be seen as weakening support for the hypothesis. Indeed, it provides additional support for a theoretical model in which exposure to violent media increases aggression (at least in part) by increasing the positivity of attitudes toward violence.

Table 5.3 displays the results of destructive testing procedures for seven separate target links. The first three involve the links between habitual exposure to violent video games (video game violence) and the three aggression measures (violence, physical aggression, verbal aggression). These analyses are the most directly relevant to the main theme of this research on violent video game effects. The next three destructive testing analyses involve the links between forgivingness and the three aggression measures. This is the first study to include trait forgivingness in a study of aggression in high school students. The large zero-order correlations with aggression, as well as the General Aggression Model, suggested that destructive testing would be useful here as well. The last destructive testing analysis involves the link between grade point average and total screen time.

Video Game Violence and Violent Behavior

The first destructive testing analysis was carried out on the link between habitual exposure to video game violence and violent behavior. When video game violence was the only predictor, it was positively linked with violence (raw $b = 0.0077$) and accounted for almost 12% of the variance in violent behavior. This link was significant, $t(184) = 4.99$, $p < 0.001$. When all variation associated with sex was first partialled out (see the "+Sex" column of Table 5.3), video game violence was still positively and significantly linked to violent behavior, although the variance uniquely attributable to video game violence dropped (as expected) to 5.20%. It is important to note that if habitual exposure to media violence does indeed cause an increase in aggressive and violent behavior, as the voluminous research literature indicates (Anderson et al., 2003), then totally partialling out sex effects from the video game violence to violent behavior link overcorrects for sex differences in exposure to violent video games and leads to an underestimation of the true video game violence effects. This is because some of the shared variance (with sex) actually belongs to video game violence. In essence, this is a very conservative estimate of the true effect of video game violence on violent behavior. It is interesting that the unique contribution of sex (after controlling for video game violence) was not significant, $F(1, 182) = 1.63$.[1]

When total screen time was added to the model there was almost no change in the video game violence slope, percentage variance uniquely attributable to video game violence, or the t-test of the video game violence slope. Total screen time did not add significantly to the prediction of violence, $F < 1$. Adding normative beliefs about aggression and positive orientation to violence to the model resulted in further decreases in the video

---

[1] The same logic applies to all predictors that share variance in predicting the criterion variable. Thus, percentage unique variance in violent behavior accounted for by video game violence when all five variables are in the model (2.65%, Table 5.3) is an extremely conservative estimate.

TABLE 5.3 Destructive testing of key theoretical links between violent video game exposure, aggressive behavior, positive orientation to violence, forgivingness, total screen time, aggression norms, sex, and GPA

Link Being Tested (Dependent Variable/Target Predictor)	Variables in the Model				
	VGV	+Sex	+TST	+Norms	+POV
Violent Behavior/Video Game Violence					
VGV slopes	.0077	.0063	.0062	.0053	.0046
% unique variance explained by VGV	11.97	5.20	5.16	3.54	2.65
t value of VGV effect	4.99*	3.29*	3.23*	2.70*	2.48*
Physical aggression/ Video Game Violence					
VGV slopes	.0260	.0165	.0158	.0132	.0105
% unique variance explained by VGV	20.71	5.49	5.03	3.30	2.08
t value of VGV effect	6.91*	3.67*	3.50*	2.87*	2.75*
Verbal aggression/ Video Game Violence					
VGV slopes	.0140	.0117	.0105	.0099	.0082
% unique variance explained by VGV	6.36	2.92	2.39	2.00	1.39
t value of VGV effect	3.53*	2.39*	2.16*	1.97*	1.72
	Forgive	+Sex	+VGV	+TST	+POV
Violence/Forgivingness					
Forgive slopes	−.1729	−.1643	−.1517	−.1622	−.1162
% unique variance explained by Forgive	10.38	9.33	7.84	8.85	4.06
t value of Forgive effect	4.60*	4.52*	4.23*	4.45*	3.13*
Physical aggression/Forgivingness					
Forgive slopes	−.5351	−.4981	−.4658	−.4849	−.2951
% unique variance explained by Forgive	15.11	13.04	11.24	12.02	3.98
t value of Forgive effect	5.71*	5.97*	5.69*	5.90*	3.93*
Verbal aggression/Forgivingness					
Forgive slopes	−.5465	−.5323	−.5121	−.5198	−.4366
% unique variance explained by Forgive	16.66	15.74	14.36	14.93	9.42
t value of Forgive effect	6.05*	5.97*	5.74*	5.90*	4.77*
	TST	+Sex	+VGV	+Norms	+POV
GPA/Total Screen Time					
TST slopes	−.0122	−.0108	−.0112	−.0112	−.0078
% unique variance explained by TST	8.46	6.05	6.40	6.38	2.98
t value of Total Screen Time effect	4.02*	3.41*	3.51*	3.51*	2.54*

*$p \leq .05$. ns = 179–185. VGV = Video Game Violence; TST = Total Screen Time; Norms = Normative Aggression Beliefs; POV = Positive Orientation towards Violence; Forgive = Forgivingness scale; GPA = Grade Point Average.

game violence effect, as expected. These two variables are also likely to be causally affected by media violence exposure, and indeed may be considered as partial mediators of media violence effects on aggression. Therefore, partialling them out of the link between video game violence and violent behavior again should be seen as a very conservative procedure. Somewhat surprisingly, the link between video game violence and violent behavior was not broken even with the addition of all these variables to the statistical model. In brief, the destructive testing procedure on the link between video game violence and violent behavior revealed it to be a remarkably strong link.

The normative beliefs measure was positively ($b = 0.0034$) related to violence even after the effects of video game violence, sex, and total screen time were statistically controlled, $F(1, 174) = 3.95$, $p < 0.05$. Similarly, positive orientation to violence was positively ($b = 0.2713$) related to violence even after the effects of video game violence, sex, total screen time, and normative beliefs were statistically controlled, $F(1, 173) = 22.84$, $p < 0.001$. The final model, with all five predictors, accounted for about 25% of the variance in violent behavior.

Video Game Violence and Physical Aggression

Destructive testing procedures on the link between video game violence and physical aggression yielded very similar results. The link did not break even when sex, total screen time, normative beliefs, and positive orientation to violence were statistically controlled (see Table 5.3). Variance in physical aggression explained by video game violence ranged from over 20% (when only video game violence was in the model) to just over 2% (when all four covariates were in the model).

The covariate effects were somewhat different for physical aggression than for violence. First, the sex effect was significant in all models, with males reporting higher levels of physical aggression than females. Second, total screen time yielded a significant positive association with physical aggression in two of the regressions: when video game violence and sex were in the model [$F(1, 175) = 4.19$, $p < 0.05$] and when video game violence, sex, and normative beliefs were in the model [$F(1, 174) = 4.16$, $p < 0.05$].

The normative beliefs and positive orientation to violence effects on physical aggression were similar to their effects on violence. Normative beliefs were positively related to physical aggression even after video game violence, sex, and total screen time were statistically controlled, $F(1, 174) = 5.93$, $p < 0.05$. Positive orientation to violence was positively related to physical aggression even after video game violence, sex, total screen time, and normative beliefs were statistically controlled, $F(1, 173)$

$= 80.49, p < 0.001$. The final model accounted for about 52% of the variance in physical aggression.

Video Game Violence and Verbal Aggression

For both theoretical and empirical reasons, we expected the link between video game violence with verbal aggression to be weaker than those with violent behavior and physical aggression. Verbal aggression is not modeled much in violent video games, and verbal aggression by the player is not rewarded in any way.

The destructive testing results confirmed this expectation. The proportion of verbal aggression uniquely associated with video game violence ranged from 6.36% to 1.39%. The positive video game violence link with verbal aggression survived the first three destructive tests (sex, total screen time, normative beliefs) but broke when positive orientation to violence was added to the model (see Table 5.3). The final model accounted for about 19% of the variance in verbal aggression.

Forgivingness and Violent Behavior, Physical Aggression, and Verbal Aggression

As noted earlier, these are the first tests of links between trait forgivingness and aggression in high school students. Section B of Table 5.3 presents the results. The forgivingness–aggression link proved to be quite strong, surviving all the destructive tests with each of the three aggression measures. Forgivingness was negatively related to all three types of aggression, accounted for 16.66% to 3.98% of the variance in the three types of aggression, and survived destructive tests that included sex, video game violence, total screen time, and positive orientation to violence. That is, participants who scored higher on trait forgivingness tended to report lower levels of aggression. The final models accounted for about 28% of the variance in violent behavior, 55% of the variance in physical aggression, and 28% of the variance in verbal aggression.

Total Screen Time and Grade Point Average

The final destructive testing analysis revealed that total screen time was negatively linked to grade point average, and that this link survived all four destructive tests. That is, participants who spent more time with screen entertainment (TV, movies, video games) had significantly lower grade point averages than those who spent less time with screen entertainment, even when sex, video game violence, normative beliefs, and positive orientation to violence were statistically controlled. The final model accounted for about 21% of the variance in grade point average.

Regression Analyses: Moderator Effects (Sex, Forgivingness, Positive
Orientation to Violence)

One question of fundamental importance for both theoretical and practical
reasons concerns who is most affected by media violence exposure. In the
present study we examined three individual differences as potential moderators of the relation between video game violence and aggression: sex,
positive orientation to violence, and forgivingness.

The results are easily summarized. Neither sex nor positive orientation
to violence interacted with video game violence for any of the three measures of aggression, all $Fs < 1.0$. Thus, the video game violence relation to
aggression was essentially the same for high school boys and girls, and for
those with a high versus low score on the positive orientation to violence
measure. Forgivingness did not interact with video game violence for the
physical or verbal aggression measures ($Fs < 1.5$, $ps > 0.2$). However, forgivingness did interact with video game violence in predicting violence,
$F(1, 181) = 5.36$, $p < 0.05$. We divided the sample into two groups at the
median forgivingness score to further explore this interaction. As anticipated, the video game violence–violent behavior slope was steeper for the
low forgivingness participants ($b = 0.0095$) than for the high forgivingness
participants ($b = 0.0027$). This indicates that the video game violence
effect on violent behavior was larger for participants who are not very
forgiving.

Overall these moderator tests suggest that no one is immune to the
aggression-enhancing effects of habitual exposure to video game violence,
but that some trait measures might mitigate the effects to some extent.
These results parallel the findings from Anderson and Dill (2000; Study
1), in which college student participants with high-trait aggression scores
displayed a larger video game violence effect on violent behavior than did
low-trait aggression participants.

Regression Analyses: Old Versus New Violent Media

The TV and movie violence exposure measures were highly correlated, $r =
0.57$, $p < 0.0001$, so they were combined to form a composite indicator of
old media violence exposure. For the 178 participants who had complete
data, this composite old media violence index was significantly correlated
with violent behavior ($r = 0.26$), physical aggression ($r = 0.36$) and verbal
aggression ($r = 0.26$). The corresponding zero-order correlations between
video game violence and the three measures of aggression were 0.36, 0.49,
and 0.27, respectively. The old media and new (video game) media vio-

lence exposure measures themselves were positively correlated as well, $r = 0.29$, $p < 0.0001$.

When both old and new violent media exposure measures were regressed on aggression, they accounted for a substantial portion of the variance in violent behavior [15.1%, $F(2, 175) = 15.50$, $p < 0.0001$], physical aggression [26.4%, $F(2, 175) = 31.42$, $p < 0.0001$], and verbal aggression [10.3%, $F(2, 175) = 10.06$, $p < 0.0001$]. Furthermore, in all three cases both types of media violence contributed significant unique increments in the prediction of aggression, Fs$(1, 175) > 5.85$, ps < 0.02.

In very conservative tests of these two media violence effects on aggression, we tested the unique increment of each in models that included sex, normative beliefs about aggression, and positive orientation toward violence as control factors. This is very conservative because theoretically two of the factors may well be mediating variables that are affected by media violence and that in turn affect aggressive behavior. In essence, these are additional destructive tests, parallel to those reported earlier.

As noted earlier, because video games model and reinforce violence and physical aggression much more than verbal aggression we expected the video game violence effect on verbal aggression to be relatively smaller. This is exactly what happened. For violent behavior, exposure to violent video games remained a significant predictor even after controlling for sex, norms, violence orientation, and old media violence exposure, $F(1, 172) = 5.46$, $p < 0.0001$, $r = 0.18$. It is interesting that the old media violence exposure link to violent behavior did not survive this destructive test, $F(1, 172) = 0.68$, ns, $r = 0.06$. The same pattern occurred for physical aggression. Exposure to violent video games remained a significant predictor [$F(1, 172) = 6.92$, $p < 0.0001$, $r = 0.20$], whereas old media violence exposure did not [$F(1, 172) = 1.01$, ns, $r = 0.08$. However, for verbal aggression, neither form of media violence exposure remained significant, Fs$(1, 172) = 2.65$ and 1.68, rs $= 0.12$ and 0.10, for new and old media violence, respectively.

Discussion

The results of this study of high school students strongly support prior correlational studies that used older (e.g., Anderson & Dill, 2000) and younger (e.g., Weigman & van Schie, 1998) populations as well as theoretical predictions that habitual exposure to violent video games will be positively correlated with high levels of aggression and violence. The present study also extends the findings of Krahé and Möller (2004) that attraction and exposure to violent video games is positively associated with norms condoning physical aggression by using a different population, a different measure of exposure to violent video games, and a different measure of aggression norms. The present study also revealed theoretically important positive associations between video game violence and other downstream variables predicted by the General Aggression Model, such as hostility, anger, and attitudes toward violence.

Three additional findings are especially important to note. First, the destructive testing analyses revealed that the video game violence effects on aggression and violence are remarkably robust, thereby ruling out a number of important alternative explanations. Second, the paucity of significant video game violence interactions with potential moderating factors reveals that large portions of the population are susceptible to violent video game effects, again replicating and extending other findings in the video game literature, as well as the larger media violence literature. Third, as in Study 1, regression results on the independent effects of new and old forms of media violence revealed larger and more robust effects for violent video game exposure than for TV and film violence. Some caution is warranted in interpreting this latter finding, because the measurement procedure used for violent video game exposure was different from that used for TV and film violence exposure.

In sum, Study 2 replicated and extended prior work in several ways, thereby providing additional support for the General Aggression Model. Study 3 was designed to fill the largest remaining gap in the violent video game research literature, the potential longitudinal effects of exposure to violent video games on children.

6

Study 3: Longitudinal Study With Elementary School Students

Study 3 was conducted to address the biggest gap in the violent video game research literature, the lack of longitudinal studies. Study 1 demonstrated that even children's games that have violent content can cause increases in aggression in the short term. Study 2 demonstrated that exposure to violent video games is associated with higher levels of aggression in the "real world" in a long-term context. Study 3 examined the longitudinal effects of high exposure to violent video games across a relatively short time span to see whether violent video game use leads to *increases* in aggressive behavior in daily life across time.

Elementary school students, their peers, and teachers were surveyed at two points during a school year. This age group was selected specifically because it was hypothesized that violent video game use might have the most noticeable effect during the middle childhood years. Because the major developmental tasks of this age group are to learn social norms of behavior and how to interact with peer groups, we hypothesized that children who were exposing themselves to high levels of violent video games would become more aggressive over the course of a school year. Aggressive behaviors are highly salient to children, so these would be measurable and might also be related to peer acceptance.

We hypothesized that children who exposed themselves to high levels of violent video games early in the school year would change to become more aggressive, and that this change would be partially mediated by hostile attribution bias. That is, controlling for prior aggressive behavior, playing violent video games would be related to later *increased* aggressive cognitions and behaviors. Furthermore, although it was not a primary objective of this study, we anticipated that if this pattern were true these children would also be more likely to be rejected by their peers. A number of control variables were also assessed to allow tests of alternative hypotheses and of some key aspects of the General Aggression Model.

Method

Participants

Four hundred thirty third- ($n = 119$), fourth- ($n = 119$), and fifth-grade ($n= 192$) students participated in the study. Students were recruited from five Minnesota schools, including one suburban private school ($n = 138$), three suburban public schools ($n = 265$), and one rural public school ($n = 27$). The sample was almost evenly divided between boys and girls, with 49% of the children being female (51% male). Participants ranged in age from 7 to 11 years ($M = 9.65$; $SD = 1.03$). Eighty-six percent of the respondents classified their ethnic background as Caucasian (which is representative of the region).

Procedure

Data were collected between November 2000 and June 2003. Interested teachers volunteered their classrooms for inclusion in the study. Each of the participating classrooms was a mandatory class (i.e., not elective) to reduce the likelihood of selection bias. Letters were sent directly to the parents of students in participating classrooms informing them about the study and requesting consent. Consent levels were at least 70% for all classrooms.

Each participant completed three confidential surveys: (1) a peer-nomination measure of aggressive and prosocial behaviors, (2) a self-report survey of media habits and demographic data, and (3) a self-report measure of hostile attribution bias. Trained research personnel administered the peer-nomination survey, and classroom teachers were trained to administer the other surveys. The surveys were administered on consecutive days. Teachers also completed one survey for each participating child, reporting on the frequency of children's aggressive and prosocial behaviors.

Each participant (including teachers) completed each of these surveys two times during the school year. The first administration (Time 1) occurred between November and February of the academic year. The second administration (Time 2) occurred between April and May of the year. The time lag between the two administrations was therefore between two and six months, and the average lag was five months.

Assessment of Social Adjustment

Peer Assessment of Social Adjustment

A peer nomination instrument was used to assess children's social adjustment, and was adapted from a peer nomination instrument that has been used in several previous studies of children's social behavior (e.g., Crick, 1995; Crick & Grotpeter, 1995). This instrument consists of 10 items. Two of these items were the peer sociometric items (nominations of liked and disliked peers), which are used extensively in research of this nature to assess peer acceptance and rejection (see Crick & Dodge, 1994, for a review). The remaining eight items assess four types of social behavior: physical aggression (two-item subscale), relational aggression (three-item subscale), prosocial behavior (two-item subscale), and verbal aggression (one item). See Table 6.1 for a listing of all items. Coefficient alpha was computed for each of the three subscales with multiple items and was found to be satisfactory, $\alpha = 0.92$ for physical aggression, 0.86 for relational aggression, and 0.80 for prosocial behavior.

TABLE 6.1   Peer nomination subscale items

Physical aggression subscale:

Who hits, kicks, or punches others?
Who pushes and shoves other kids around?

Relational aggression subscale:

Who tries to make another kid not like a certain person by spreading rumors about that person or talking behind his or her back?
Who, when they are mad at a person, gets even by keeping that person from being in their group of friends?
Who, when they are mad at a person, ignores the person or stops talking to him or her?

Verbal aggression item:

Who says mean things to other kids to insult them or put them down?

Prosocial behavior subscale:

Who does nice things for others?
Who tries to cheer up other kids who are upset or sad about something? They try to make the kids feel happy again.

Teacher Ratings of Social Adjustment

Teachers completed a survey assessing children's aggression and prosocial behavior. This instrument consists of twelve behavioral subscales, including a variety of behaviors (e.g. aggressive behavior, victimization, prosocial behavior, and others). For the purposes of this study, only the subscales reflecting relational aggression, physical aggression, and prosocial behavior were used in subsequent analyses. These items are listed in Table 6.2. Coefficient alpha was computed and found to be satisfactory for each subscale: $\alpha = 0.92$ for teacher ratings of relational aggression, 0.92 for teacher ratings of physical aggression, and 0.91 for teacher ratings of prosocial behavior.

Self-Report of Fights

One item asked how many physical fights the participants had been in during the school year.

Assessment of Media Habits

Violent Media Exposure

Similar to Anderson and Dill's (2000) approach (and our Study 1), participants were asked to name their three favorite television shows, their

Table 6.2   Teacher rating subscale items

Physical aggression subscale:

This child hits or kicks peers.
This child initiates or gets into physical fights with peers.
This child threatens to hit or beat up other children.
This child pushes or shoves peers.

Relational aggression subscale:

When this child is mad at a peer, she or he gets even by excluding the peer from his or her clique or playgroup.
This child spreads rumors or gossips about some peers.
When angry at a peer, this child tries to get other children to stop playing with the peer or to stop liking the peer.
This child threatens to stop being a peer's friend in order to hurt the peer or to get what she or he wants from the peer.
When mad at a peer, this child ignores the peer or stops talking to the peer.

Prosocial behavior subscale:

This child says supportive things to peers.
This child tries to cheer up peers when they are upset or sad about something.
This child is helpful to peers.
This child is kind to peers.

---

three favorite video or computer games, and their three favorite movies or videos. For each named media product, participants were asked to rate how frequently they watched or played on a five-point scale (1 = "Almost never," 5 = "Almost every day"). Participants were also asked to rate how violent they consider each media product to be on a four-point scale (1 = "Not at all violent," 4 = "Very violent"). A violence exposure score was computed for each participant by multiplying the frequency of watching or playing each media product by its subjective violence rating, and then taking the mean of the three similar products. Accordingly, media-specific (i.e., violent TV exposure, violent video game exposure, and violent movies and videos exposure) violence exposure scores were computed for each participant. Finally, an overall violent media exposure score, the mean of all nine products (TV, video games, movies and videos), was also calculated. Coefficient alpha was computed for the overall media violence exposure scale and found to be modest but sufficient for a large sample study ($\alpha = 0.68$).[1]

Previous research has demonstrated that people assess the violence in media products based on the amount of physical violence, rather than relational aggression. Potter (1999) found that violence ratings were most strongly correlated with the graphicness of the portrayal of physical violence, across age, sex, amount of television viewing, and other factors.

Amount of Television Watching and Video Game Play

Participants reported the amount of time they spent watching television and playing video games during different periods on weekdays and weekends. Weekly amounts were calculated from these responses.

Assessment of Hostile Attribution Bias and Social Information Processing

The final survey was an adapted version of a hostile attribution survey that has been reliably used in past research (e.g., Crick, 1995; Nelson & Crick, 1999). This instrument is comprises 10 stories, each describing an instance of provocation in which the intent of the provocateur is ambiguous. The stories were developed to reflect common situations that children and

---

[1] It is unclear why one should expect the overall media violence exposure scale or the specific media violence exposure scales to have high internal reliability. Calculating violence exposure from favorite games appears to be an empirically appropriate approach. However, it is entirely likely that some children would like both violent and nonviolent games, which would make the scale appear unreliable, when in fact the scale is measuring exactly what it is intended to measure—that some people watch and play primarily violent media, some watch and play primarily nonviolent media, and some watch and play a mix of violent and nonviolent media.

young adolescents might encounter in the school years. Four of the stories depict physical provocations and six represent relational provocations. Participants answer two questions following each story. The first presents four possible reasons for the peer's behavior, two of which indicate hostile intent and two reflect benign intent. The second question asks whether the provocateur(s) intended to be mean or not. This survey assesses the participant's perception of hostility from the outside world. Two scale scores result from analysis of this measure: intent attributions for relational provocation and intent attributions for physical provocations. One example of each type is shown below.

Physical Provocation Example.   Imagine that you are sitting at a table in the cafeteria, eating lunch. You look up and see another student you recognize coming over to your table with a large carton of milk. You turn around to eat your lunch, and the next thing you know the student spills the milk all over your back. The back of your shirt is completely soaked.

1. Why did the student spill the milk all over your back?
   a. The student just slipped on something.
   b. The student does stupid things like that sometimes.
   c. The student wanted to make me mad.
   d. The student wasn't looking where they were going.
2. In this situation, do you think that the student was
   a. deliberately trying to be mean?
   b. just being thoughtless, but not deliberately trying to be mean?

Relational Provocation Example.   Imagine that you are standing in the hallway one morning before class. As you are standing there, two students from your class walk by. As they walk by you, they look at you, whisper something to each other and then they laugh.

1. Why did the two students laugh when they walked by you?
   a. The students were "bad mouthing" me (spreading rumors).
   b. The students were laughing at a joke that one of them told.
   c. The students were just having fun.
   d. The students were trying to make me mad.
2. In this situation, do you think that the two students were
   a. deliberately trying to be mean?
   b. just being thoughtless, but not deliberately trying to be mean?

Based on procedures delineated by Fitzgerald and Asher (1987), the children's responses to the attribution assessments were summed within and across the stories for each provocation type. Each item was scored as a one if the participant selected a hostile intent, or as a zero if not. Possible scores ranged from 0 through 12 (0–8 for the physical aggression subscale and 0–12 for the relational subscale). Finally, coefficient alpha was computed for each of these scales and found to be satisfactory: intent attributions for relational provocations ($\alpha = 0.83$), intent attributions for physical provocations ($\alpha = 0.75$), and overall hostile attribution ($\alpha = 0.85$).

Composite Measures

Composite measures of physical and relational aggression were created because we had multiple informants of those variables. Peer ratings of physical aggression, teacher ratings of physical aggression, and self-reports of physical fights were standardized and averaged to create a physical aggression composite. Some versions of the survey (approximately 40 surveys) asked whether participants had been involved in physical fights during the school year rather than asking how many physical fights the participants had been in. All self-report fight data were reduced to dichotomous data (yes or no fights) to make the versions compatible.

Peer ratings and teacher ratings of relational aggression were standardized and averaged to create a relational aggression composite. Coefficient alpha was computed for each of these scales and found to be satisfactory: the physical aggression scale at Time 1 ($\alpha = 0.87$), the physical aggression scale at Time 2 ($\alpha = 0.89$), the relational aggression scale at Time 1 ($\alpha = 0.90$), and the relational aggression scale at Time 2 ($\alpha = 0.91$).

Standardized ratings of peer acceptance were reverse-scored and averaged with standardized ratings of peer rejection to create a single peer rejection composite. These items were significantly correlated with each other, but only yielded alphas of 0.54 for Time 1 and 0.57 for Time 2, probably because this scale only comprised two items.

Results: Correlational Analyses

At Time 1 children reported spending an average of 20.8 hours per week watching television ($SD = 13.9$), and 9.6 hours per week playing video games ($SD = 11.6$). These averages mask important sex-correlated differences, however. Third- through fifth-grade boys watched more television ($M = 22.6$, $SD = 13.9$) than girls ($M = 19.0$, $SD = 13.6$; $t(414) = 2.6$, $p < 0.01$). Boys also played video games for significantly more time ($M = 13.4$, $SD = 13.5$) than girls ($M = 5.9$, $SD = 7.8$; $t(407) = 6.8$, $p < 0.001$).

STUDY 3 IN A NUTSHELL

Who Did What?

We gave surveys to 430 third, fourth, and fifth graders, their peers, and their teachers at two times during a school year. From children themselves, we measured (1) their violent TV, movie, and video game exposure, (2) whether they see the world in aggressive terms, and (3) whether they had been involved in physical fights this year. From peers we measured (1) which children were verbally aggressive, (2) relationally aggressive, (3) physically aggressive, or were (4) positive and prosocial in their behaviors, as well as (5) which children they liked or disliked. From teachers we measured children's (1) relational aggression, (2) physical aggression, (3) positive prosocial behaviors, and (4) school performance.

What Did We Expect?

We expected that children who played a greater number of violent video games early in the school year would change to see the world as more of a hostile place, and would in turn change to become more aggressive and less prosocial, which in turn would be related to them being more rejected by their peers. Once again, the study was designed such that children who played more violent video games could also become less aggressive over time (which would be evidence for catharsis).

What Did We Actually Find?

We found what we expected—children who played more violent video games early in the school year changed to see the world in a more aggressive way and also changed to become more verbally and physically aggressive later in the school year. Higher aggression and lower prosocial behavior were in turn related to children being more rejected by their peers.

What Surprised Us?

We were surprised to find measurable changes in aggressive behavior in such a short time (average lag between measurements was 5 months). It was also surprising that the peers and teachers noticed the changes, especially since they do not know what the children do when they're not at school.

We were again somewhat surprised that there was no apparent difference between boys and girls, children who had high or low hostile attribution biases, or children who already had or had not gotten into physical fights. Again, many people have assumed that boys who are already aggressive are more vulnerable to media violence effects, but it seems that all groups are equally affected.

(continued)

What Worries Us?

It appears that no one is truly "immune" from the effects of media violence exposure.

What Gives Us Hope?

Again, parents seem to be in a powerful position. Setting limits on the amount and content of screen media appears to be a protective factor for children.

What Else Did We Find?

Screen time (TV and video game time combined) was a significant negative predictor of grades. That is, the more time children spend in front of a screen, the worse their school performance. We also found evidence that *amount* and *content* of media have different effects. *Amount* of screen time affects school performance, but not aggressive behavior, whereas violent *content* of media affects aggressive behavior, but not school performance. We also found some evidence that the relation between violent video game exposure and physically aggressive behavior may be stronger than the relation between violent TV and movie exposure and physical aggression.

Single Point in Time Correlations

The first column of Table 6.3 presents the results from the first measurement. At Time 1, video game violence exposure (VGV) was significantly positively correlated with hostile attribution bias, verbal aggression, and physical aggression. Video game violence was significantly negatively correlated with prosocial behavior. Video game violence was not significantly related to relational aggression; this was not unexpected because relational aggression is not a part of violent video games. The Time 2 results (column 2 of Table 6.3) were essentially the same.

Table 6.4 presents correlations between total screen time (TST), video game violence, and school performance. Total screen time was negatively correlated with grades at both Time 1 and Time 2. Video game violence was less strongly (but significantly) negatively correlated with grades at Time 1, and was not significantly correlated with grades at Time 2. Overall, these cross-sectional results closely replicate other correlational studies in the video game violence literature.

TABLE 6.3   Correlations between video game violence exposure and hostile attributions, aggressive behaviors, and prosocial behaviors

Outcome Variables	1 Time 1 Video Game Violence with Time 1 Outcomes	2 Time 2 Video Game Violence with Time 2 Outcomes	3 Time 1 Video Game Violence with Time 2 Outcomes	4 Time 2 Video Game Violence with Time 1 Outcome
Hostile attribution				
Overall hostile attribution	.15**	.22***	.24***	.13*
Relational hostile attribution	.12*	.19***	.22***	.13*
Physical hostile attribution	.15**	.20***	.20***	.09
Aggressive behaviors				
Verbal aggression (peer) nomination	.22***	.27***	.28***	.17*
Relational aggression (peer) & teacher nomination	.04	.06	−.02	.04
Physical aggression (self-report, peer & teacher nomination)	.35***	.40***	.40***	.28***
Prosocial behaviors				
Prosocial behavior (peer & teacher nomination)	−.32***	−.28***	−.30***	−.29***

$^+p < .10$, $^*p < .05$, $^{**}p < .01$, $^{***}p < .001$

TABLE 6.4   Intercorrelations between total screen time and violent video game exposure, with school performance

	Grades (T1)	Grades (T2)
Total Screen Time (T1)	−.22 ***	−.20 ***
Total Screen Time (T2)	−.20 ***	−.16 **
Video Game Violence (T1)	−.16 **	−.15 **
Video Game Violence (T2)	−.10 +	−.08

$+p < .10$, $^*p < .05$, $^{**}p < .01$, $^{***}p < .001$.

Lagged Correlations: Looking Forward and Backward in Time

The most important correlations appear in the third column of Table 6.3, which presents correlations between Time 1 video game violence and Time 2 outcome variables. Time 1 video game violence exposure significantly predicted Time 2 hostile attribution bias, both verbal and physical aggression, and prosocial behavior. These are the first longitudinal tests of the hypothesis that frequent exposure to violent video games leads to increases in physical aggression, increases in cognitive precursors of such aggression (e.g., hostile attributions), and decreases in prosocial behavior.

The fourth column of Table 6.3 presents correlations between Time 1 variables and Time 2 video game violence. The Time 1 "outcome" measures of hostile attribution bias, verbal aggression, physical aggression, and prosocial behavior all correlated significantly with Time 2 video game violence.

Total screen time at Time 1 was significantly negatively correlated with grades at Time 2, and total screen time at Time 2 was similarly correlated with grades at Time 1 (Table 6.4). Video game violence at Time 1 was again less strongly (but significantly) negatively correlated with grades at Time 2, whereas Time 2 video game violence was only marginally significantly correlated with grades at Time 1.

It is interesting that all the Column 4 cross-lagged correlations were substantially smaller than the corresponding longitudinal correlations in Column 3, with two exceptions: the video game violence/prosocial behavior and the total screen time/grades correlations were essentially equivalent. Overall, the two sets of lagged correlations strongly support the hypothesis that frequent exposure to violent video games causes later increases in aggression, and contradict the alternative hypothesis that the typical cross-sectional correlation between video game violence exposure and physical aggression is a mere artifact of inherently violent people choosing violent video games.

Results: Regression Analyses

Destructive Testing

As shown in Table 6.3, the correlation between Time 1 exposure to violent video games and Time 2 relational aggression was not significant; therefore, destructive testing of this effect was not needed. However, four target links involving Time 1 video game violence were suitable for destructive testing. These are the links with hostile attribution bias, verbal aggression, physical aggression, and prosocial behavior (all at Time 2). The relevant competitor variables were sex, amount of lag between Time 1 and Time 2, race (dichotomously coded as white or minority), total screen time at Time 1 (normalized by conducting a square root transformation to correct for a high degree of skew), hostile attribution bias at Time 1, and parental involvement. For each dependent variable (e.g., Time 2 physical aggression) the Time 1 measure of that variable was included as the final competitor variable added to the destructive testing set. This allows a more stringent test of the longitudinal hypotheses. For example, by adding Time 1 physical aggression to the destructive test of the link between Time 1 video game violence and Time 2 physical aggression, we are in essence examining the change in physical aggression scores at Time 2 brought about by Time 1 video game violence. This is, however, a very conservative test. If video game violence is causally related to aggressive behaviors, for example, then controlling for earlier aggressive behavior also partially controls for earlier video game violence, which constitutes an overcorrection.

One additional destructive test was conducted on the link between total screen time (TST) at Time 1 and school performance at Time 2. Time 1 video game violence was used as a competitor variable in this analysis instead of Time 1 total screen time. Table 6.5 displays these results.

Video Game Violence and Hostile Attribution Bias

The first destructive testing analysis was conducted on the link between Time 1 exposure to violent video games and Time 2 hostile attribution bias (HAB; Table 6.5-A). When Time 1 video game violence was the only predictor, it was positively linked with later hostile attribution bias, accounting for 5.5% of the variance in hostile attribution bias. This link was significant [$t(304) = 4.20, p < 0.001$]. When all variation with sex was partialled out (that is, sex was added to the statistical model, see the +Sex column of Table 6.5, part A), video game violence was still significantly linked to hostile attribution bias and the variance uniquely attributable to video game violence did not substantially change (as would be predicted, given that both boys and girls are equally likely to have a hostile attribution bias). Neither the addition of the lag time (the +Lag column) nor the race variables (+Race column) to the statistical model substantially affected the unique effect of video game violence on hostile attribution bias.

When all variation with total screen time was additionally partialled out (the +TST column), video game violence continued to be significantly linked to hostile attribution bias although the variance uniquely attributable to video game violence dropped (as predicted) to 4.2%. Because total screen time is significantly and positively correlated with violence exposure, this probably overcorrects for the effect of pure screen time and underestimates the effect of video game violence. The inclusion of parental involvement at Time 1 (the +PI column) did not change the relation between video game violence and hostile attribution bias.

Finally, when the variation with Time 1 hostile attribution bias was partialled out, video game violence continued to be significantly linked to Time 2 hostile attribution bias, although the unique variance attributable to video game violence dropped (again as predicted) to 2.0%. Similarly, because hostile attribution bias is predicted to be modified by video game violence and may also contribute to seeking out video game violence, controlling for Time 1 hostile attribution bias should be seen as a very conservative procedure. Perhaps surprisingly, the video game violence–hostile attribution bias link was not broken even with the inclusion of these six competitor variables to the statistical model. In brief, the destructive testing procedure on the link between video game violence and hostile attribution bias revealed it to be a surprisingly strong link. The final model, with all seven predictors, accounted for 47% of the variance in hostile attribution bias at Time 2.

Video Game Violence and Verbal Aggression

The destructive testing analysis on the link between Time 1 exposure to violent video games and Time 2 verbal aggression also yielded surprisingly strong results (Table 6.5-B). When Time 1 video game violence was the only predictor, it was positively linked with later verbal aggression and accounted for 7.2% of the variance. This link was significant [$t(321) = 4.99$, $p < 0.001$]. When variation with sex was first partialled out, video game violence was still significantly linked to verbal aggression, although the amount of variance uniquely attributable to video game violence dropped to 4.9% (as would be predicted, given that boys tend to play more violent video games). Adding further controls for amount of lag time and race did not substantially change the relation between video game violence and verbal aggression.

When all variation with total screen time was partialled out, the video game violence link was reduced to 3.7% of unique variance but was still significant. When hostile attribution bias and parental involvement were additionally partialled out, video game violence was still significantly linked to verbal aggression, although the variance uniquely attributable to video game violence dropped to 3.1%.

Finally, when the variation with Time 1 verbal aggression was partialled out, video game violence remained significantly linked to Time 2 verbal aggression, although the unique variance attributable to video game violence dropped (again as predicted) to 1.0%. Again, because aggressive behaviors are predicted by video game violence and predict video game

TABLE 6.5 Destructive testing of key theoretical links between violent video game exposure, hostile attribution bias, verbal aggression, relational aggression, physical aggression, prosocial behavior, total screen time, and grades.

Link Being Tested (Dependent Variable/Target Predictor)	VGV	+Sex	+Lag	+Race	+TST	+PI	+HA1
			Variables in the Model				
A.							
Hostile Attribution (T2)/VGV(T1)							
Video Game Violence slopes	.022	.024	.024	.024	.020	.019	.013
% unique variance explained by VGV	5.5	6.3	6.1	6.1	4.2	3.8	2.0
t value of VGV effect	4.20*	4.04*	3.92*	3.92*	3.11*	2.97*	2.76*

	VGV	+Sex	+Lag	+Race	+TST	+HA1	+PI	+VA1
B.								
Verbal Aggression (T2)/VGV(T1)								
Video Game Violence slopes	.090	.074	.075	.075	.065	.059	.059	.034
% unique variance explained by VGV	7.2	4.9	5.0	5.0	3.7	3.1	3.1	1.0
t value of VGV effect	4.99*	3.69*	3.69*	3.70*	3.03*	2.78*	2.76*	2.01*

	VGV	+Sex	+Lag	+Race	+TST	+HA1	+PI	+PA1
C.								
Physical Aggression (T2)/VGV(T1)								
Video Game Violence slopes	.103	.077	.080	.080	.080	.077	.077	.049
% unique variance explained by VGV	15.8	8.8	9.6	9.7	9.6	8.8	8.9	3.6
t value of VGV effect	7.61*	5.23*	5.40*	5.44*	5.12*	4.95*	4.93*	3.90*

	VGV	+Sex	+Lag	+Race	+TST	+HA1	+PI	+Pro1
D.								
Prosocial Behavior (T2)/VGV(T1)								
Video Game Violence slopes	-8.0	-6.0	-5.7	-5.7	-5.3	-5.0	-4.4	-0.7
% unique variance explained by VGV	8.0	4.5	4.0	4.0	3.5	3.2	2.4	0.1
t value of VGV effect	-5.14*	-3.49*	-3.26*	-3.25*	-2.95*	-2.97*	-2.45*	-0.54

	TST	+Sex	+Lag	+Race	+VGV	+HA1	+PI	+Grd1
E.								
Grades in School (T2)/TST(T1)								
Total Screen Time slopes	-.019	-.020	-.020	-.020	-.017	-.017	-.017	.002
% unique variance explained by TST	4.5	5.0	5.0	4.8	3.6	3.5	3.5	0.0
t value of TST effect	-3.72*	-3.85*	-3.19*	-3.87*	-3.23*	-3.15*	-3.17*	0.57

*$p \leq .05$. $ns = 299 - 321$. VGV = Video game violence; TST = Total Screen Time; PI = Parental Involvement in Media; HA = Hostile Attribution Bias; VA = Verbal Aggression; PA = Physical Aggression; Pro = Prosocial Behavior; Grd = Grades in School; T1 = Time 1; T2 = Time 2.

violence, controlling for Time 1 verbal aggression is likely to be a conservative procedure. Nonetheless, the link between video game violence and verbal aggression was not broken even with the inclusion of all seven competitor variables to the statistical model. The destructive testing procedure on the video game violence–verbal aggression link revealed it to be a strong link. The final model, with all eight predictors, accounted for 48% of the variance in verbal aggression at Time 2.

Video Game Violence and Physical Aggression

A destructive testing analysis was conducted on the link between Time 1 exposure to violent video games and Time 2 physical aggression (Table 6.5-C). When Time 1 video game violence was the only predictor, it was positively linked with later physical aggression and accounted for almost 16% of the variance. This link was significant [$t(309) = 7.61, p < 0.001$]. When all variation with sex was first partialled out, video game violence was still significantly linked to physical aggression, although the amount of variance uniquely attributable to video game violence dropped to 8.8% (as predicted, given that boys tend to play more violent video games and tend to display more physical aggression). Controlling for amount of lag time, race, total screen time, hostile attribution bias, and parental involvement at Time 1 did not substantially change the relation between video game violence and physical aggression.

Finally, when the variation with Time 1 physical aggression was partialled out, video game violence continued to be significantly linked to Time 2 physical aggression, although the unique variance attributable to Time 1 video game violence dropped (as predicted) to 3.6%. Once again, because aggressive behaviors are predicted by video game violence and predict video game violence, controlling for Time 1 physical aggression is likely to be a conservative procedure. The link between video game violence and physical aggression was not broken even with the inclusion of these seven theoretically relevant variables to the statistical model. The destructive testing procedure on the link between video game violence and physical aggression revealed it to be quite strong. The final model, with all eight predictors, accounted for 52% of the variance in physical aggression at Time 2.

Video Game Violence and Prosocial Behavior

A destructive testing analysis was conducted on the link between Time 1 exposure to violent video games and Time 2 prosocial behavior (Table 6.5-D). When Time 1 video game violence was the only predictor, it was negatively linked with later prosocial behavior and accounted for 8% of the variance. This link was significant [$t(303) = -5.14, p < 0.001$). When all variation with sex was partialled out, video game violence was still significantly linked to prosocial behavior, although the amount of variance uniquely attributable to video game violence dropped to 4.5% (as predicted). Controlling for amount of lag time, race, and total screen time lowered the amount of variance in prosocial behavior uniquely attributed to video game violence to 3.5%.

When all variation with hostile attribution bias was partialled out, video game violence continued to be significantly linked to prosocial behavior, although the variance uniquely attributable to video game violence dropped (as predicted) to 3.2%. The inclusion of parental involvement at Time 1 further reduced the unique effect of Time 1 video game violence on later prosocial behavior to 2.4%.

When the variation with Time 1 prosocial behavior was partialled out, the link between video game violence and prosocial behavior was finally broken, with Time 1 video game violence uniquely accounting for only 0.1% of the variance in Time 2 prosocial behavior. Because prosocial behaviors are predicted by video game violence, it is perhaps not surprising that the link was broken with the inclusion of prior prosocial behaviors.

Overall, the destructive testing procedure on the link between video game violence and prosocial behavior revealed it to be a strong link, although not as strong as the links of video game violence with hostile attribution bias, verbal aggression, and physical aggression. The final model, with all eight predictors, accounted for 54% of the variance in prosocial behavior at Time 2.

Total Screen Time and School Performance.

A destructive testing analysis was conducted on the link between Time 1 total screen time (TST) and Time 2 grades (Table 6.5-E). When Time 1 total screen time was the only predictor, it was negatively linked with later grades, and accounted for 4.5% of the variance. This link was significant $[t(298) = -3.72, p < 0.001)$. When all variation with sex, lag, and race was partialled out, total screen time was still significantly linked to grades, and the amount of variance uniquely attributable to total screen time was substantially unchanged. Controlling for amount of Time 1 video game violence, hostile attribution bias, and parental involvement lowered the amount of variance in grades uniquely attributed to total screen time to 3.5%, still statistically significant.

When the variation with Time 1 grades was partialled out, the link between total screen time and grades was finally broken. Because grades are likely to be relatively stable over a school year and are also predicted by total screen time, it is not surprising that the link was broken with the inclusion of earlier grades. As with the longitudinal link between video game violence and prosocial behavior, this breaking of the link between total screen time and grades could indicate either the use of an overly conservative testing procedure that simply failed to "reveal" a true causal effect or the possibility that total screen time is not causally related to school performance. Overall, the destructive testing procedure on the link between total screen time and school performance revealed it to be a strong link. The final model, with all eight predictors, accounted for 76% of the variance in grades at Time 2.

Path Analyses

Path analyses were conducted to test our hypothesized model of the direction of effects. Based on earlier studies (e.g., Anderson & Dill, 2000; Gentile et al., 2004), we hypothesized that the amount and the content of media exposure would have differential impacts. We expected that greater amounts of time viewing screen-based media (TV, videos, DVDs, and video games) would have a direct effect on school performance but would not be as directly related to aggressive behaviors. Greater exposure to violent video games was predicted to have a direct effect on physical aggression and prosocial behaviors (increasing and decreasing effects, respectively), but would not have a direct effect on school performance. Because violent video games contain much physical aggression, little verbal aggression, and almost no relational aggression, we expected video game violence exposure to have relatively smaller (or no) effects on verbal and relational aggression than on physical aggression.

Furthermore, violent content was also predicted to increase hostile attribution biases, which in turn would also mediate the effects between exposure to violent video games and aggressive and prosocial behaviors. Parent involvement in children's media was hypothesized to reduce aggressive and increase prosocial behaviors. Sex was also hypothesized to be related to the expression of aggressive and prosocial behaviors, in that girls were expected to exhibit more verbal and relational aggression, as well as more prosocial behavior, but boys were expected to exhibit more physical aggression. Finally, it was hypothesized that more aggressive and fewer prosocial behaviors would predict greater peer rejection.

Because this was a longitudinal study, our hypotheses were time-based as well. Children who play more violent video games early in the school year were hypothesized to have greater hostile attribution biases, and these biases were expected to lead to increases in aggressive behavior. In short, we expected hostile attribution biases to at least partially mediate the longitudinal effects of early exposure to violent video games. Therefore, the path analysis included total screen time, video game violence exposure, parent involvement, and sex as variables at Time 1. Because we expected hostile attribution bias to mediate the effects, but we only had measures from two points in time, we entered a mean of Time 1 and Time 2 hostile attribution bias scores. This was done because theoretically we expect that a change in hostile attribution bias should typically precede changes in aggressive behavior, and therefore including the average between Time 1 and Time 2 is most theoretically appropriate.[2] School performance, verbal aggression, physical aggression, relational aggression, and prosocial behavior were Time 2 variables, as was the peer rejection variable.[3]

As can be seen in Figure 6.1, each of our hypotheses was confirmed. Statistically significant pathways are displayed, with the standardized regression coefficients presented—note that each of these coefficients can be interpreted as a partial correlation controlling for each of the other variables included in the model. Video game violence exposure and total screen time both increased hostile attribution bias, which in turn was related to increased verbal, physical, and relational aggressive behavior, as well as to decreased prosocial behavior. Verbal aggression and prosocial behavior were in turn related to Time 2 peer rejection. Video game violence exposure was also directly related (over and above the mediated path via hostile attribution bias) to significantly increased verbal aggression, increased physical aggression, and significantly decreased prosocial behavior. Having more involved parents resulted in children showing more prosocial behavior. Also, as was predicted, boys were more likely to be physically aggressive, and girls were more likely to be relationally aggressive and more prosocial toward their peers. The full intercorrelation matrix is shown in Table 6.6.

A second path analysis was conducted looking solely at physical aggression at Time 2 as the dependent variable (Figure 6.2). Again, it was predicted that hostile attribution bias would mediate the relationship between violent video game exposure at Time 1 and physically aggressive behavior at Time 2. Similarly, it was predicted that video game violence would also contribute directly to later aggressive behavior. In contrast to Figure 6.1, this path analysis included physical aggression at Time 1.

[2] Although using the mean is most theoretically appropriate, the path analyses were essentially the same whether Time 1, Time 2, or a mean of Time 1 and Time 2 hostile attribution bias was used.

[3] One school was surveyed twice, two years apart. Therefore, 26 children are included as both third graders and fifth graders. Analyses removing these children as fifth graders showed no substantive differences in the path analyses. If there is any bias, it is likely that the second time children participated in the study, they may have figured out what we were studying and would give more socially acceptable answers, which would only serve to reduce our ability to find significant effects. They were therefore left in to increase the generalizeability and power of the analyses.

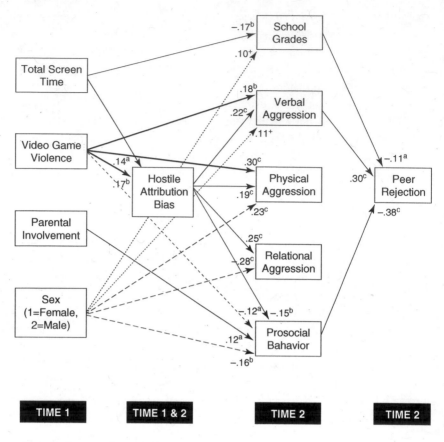

Figure 6.1 Path analysis model of all key variables.

As shown in Figure 6.2, our hypotheses were confirmed. Physically aggressive behavior at Time 1 was related to increased hostile attribution bias, which in turn was related to increased physically aggressive behavior at Time 2. In addition, as predicted, physically aggressive behavior at Time 1 also directly predicted physically aggressive behavior at Time 2, capturing a great deal of the variance (*beta* = 0.59). Nonetheless, video game violence exposure increased hostile attribution bias and also contributed directly to Time 2 physical aggression, even controlling for total screen time, parental involvement, sex, Time 1 physical aggression, and hostile attribution bias.

TABLE 6.6 Intercorrelations between predictor and outcome variables in the path analysis ($N = 304$)

	Time 1 Variables				T1 & T2		Time 2 Variables			
	TST-T1	VGV-T1	PIIM-T1	Sex	HAB	GPA	VA	PA	RA	PB
1. Total screen time (T1)										
2. Video game violence (T1)	.35c									
3. Parent involvement in Media (T1)	.01	-.14a								
4. Sex (1=Female, 2=Male)	.24c	.44c	-.10+							
5. Hostile Att Bias (T1/T2)	.19c	.22c	-.07	.08						
6. School Performance (T2)	-.20c	-.14a	.03	.01	-.14a					
7. Verbal Aggression (T2)	.17b	.29c	-.04	.22c	.27c	-.24c				
8. Physical Aggression (T2)	.16b	.42c	-.06	.36c	.26c	-.21c	.65c			
9. Relational Aggression (T2)	-.05	-.04	.08	-.25c	.22c	-.18b	.49c	.36c		
10. Prosocial Behaviors (T2)	-.17b	-.28c	.17b	-.26c	-.21c	.35c	-.37c	-.46c	-.34c	
11. Peer Rejection (T2)	.10+	.07	-.10+	.04	.14a	-.28c	.41c	.29c	.33c	-.48c

Note: $^+ p < .10$, $^a p < .05$, $^b p < .01$, $^c p < .001$. T1 = Time 1; T2 = Time 2; Att = Attribution.

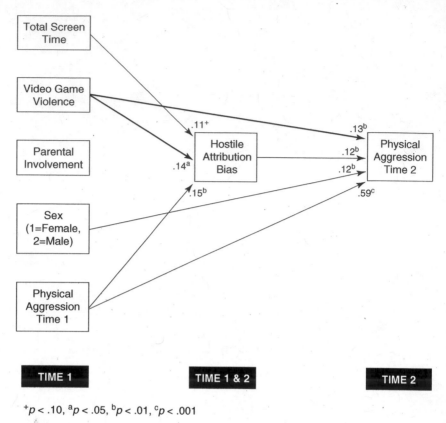

TIME 1   TIME 1 & 2   TIME 2

$^+p < .10, {}^ap < .05, {}^bp < .01, {}^cp < .001$

Figure 6.2 Path analysis model of video game violence exposure at Time 1 on physical aggression at Time 2, controlling for physical aggression at Time 1 ($N = 347$).

Regression Analyses: Old Versus New Violent Media

The TV and movie violence exposure measures were again combined to form a composite indicator of old media violence exposure. For the 429 participants who had complete data, this composite old media violence index was significantly correlated with verbal aggression ($r = 0.23$), physical aggression ($r = 0.36$), and prosocial behavior ($r = -0.31$). The corresponding zero-order correlations between video game violence were 0.22, 0.35, and –0.32, respectively. The old media and new (video game) media violence exposure measures themselves were positively correlated as well, $r = 0.54, p < 0.0001$.

When both old and new Time 1 violent media exposure measures were regressed on Time 2 physical aggression, they both independently accounted for a substantial portion of the variance (TV/movie: $F(1, 361) = 20.3$, $p < 0.001$, $b = .111$, $r = 0.23$; video games: $F(1, 361) = 21.6$, $p < 0.001$, $b = 0.073$, $r = 0.24$). After controlling for Time 1 physical aggression, both old and new media violence exposure still significantly predicted Time 2 physical aggression. In a more conservative test of these two media's violence effects on physical aggression, we first statistically controlled for Time 1 physical aggression, Time 1 total screen time, Time 1 parental involvement in media, Time 1 hostile attribution bias, sex, race, and school lag. We then simultaneously tested the unique variance in physical aggression accounted for by Time 1 violent video game exposure and Time 1 violent TV/movie exposure. The Time 1 video game violence effect remained a significant predictor of Time 2 physical aggression ($F(1, 310) = 7.38$, $p < 0.001$, $b = 0.038$, $r = 0.15$) even after controlling for violent TV/movie exposure. However, the TV/movie violence effect became nonsignificant. This does not mean that TV/movie violence does not contribute to increases in physical aggression over time. A more appropriate interpretation is that the video game violence effect was more robust, and that the high correlation between video game and TV/movie violence exposure overwhelmed the unique effect of TV/movie violence in this conservative statistical procedure.

As noted earlier, because video games model and reinforce violence and physical aggression much more than verbal aggression and relational aggression, we expected the video game violence effect on verbal and relational aggression to be relatively smaller. This is exactly what was found. For verbal aggression, both Time 1 TV/movie and video game violence predicted Time 2 verbal aggression (*beta* = 0.20, $p < 0.001$ and *beta* = 0.17, $p < 0.01$, respectively). When Time 1 verbal aggression was added, TV/movie violence remained significant (*beta* = 0.10, $p < 0.05$), but video game violence became marginally significant. When all other predictors were added, both old and new media became nonsignificant, though their joint contribution remained significant [$F(2, 312) = 3.68$, $p < 0.05$, $r = 0.11$).

For relational aggression, neither old nor new media violence exposure at Time 1 significantly predicted Time 2 relational aggression. For prosocial behavior, both Time 1 TV/movie and VG violence negatively predict Time 2 prosocial behavior (TV/movie: $F(1,355) = 12.04$, $p < 0.01$, $r = 0.18$; video game: $F(1, 355) = 8.14$, $p < 0.01$, $r = 0.15$). However, prosocial behavior appeared to be very stable across time (*beta* = 0.70, $p < 0.001$). Once Time 1 prosocial behavior was entered, both old and new media violence exposure added very little additional predictive power and were nonsignificant, individually and jointly. However, it is important to recall that the path analysis did reveal a significant effect of Time 1 video game violence on prosocial behavior, both directly and indirectly through hostile attribution bias (see Figure 6.1).

Discussion

Study 3 is the first longitudinal study of violent video game effects on aggressive behavior. The length of the longitudinal aspect was relatively short (2–6 months) compared to some longitudinal studies in the television violence domain (e.g., over 15 years). Indeed, one of our concerns at the outset was that this time interval might well have been too short for video game violence effects to appear. Nonetheless, sizeable effects did occur. For example, exposure to violent video games at Time 1 correlated at $r = 0.40$ with physical aggression at Time 2. The longitudinal path analyses demonstrated that this significant relation held up even when a host of Time 1 and Time 2 variables (e.g., Time 1 physical aggressiveness) were statistically controlled. In a sense, Study 3 closes the third side of the major methods triangle: for the first time, there is experimental, cross-sectional, and longitudinal evidence concerning the hypothesis that exposure to violent video games can cause increases in the likelihood of aggressive behavior.

Study 3 demonstrated several other effects of repeated exposure to violent video games, specifically, increases in hostile attribution bias and verbal aggression and decreases in prosocial behavior. It also demonstrated a link between total screen time and declines in school performance. Several mediational links through hostile attribution bias were established, linking Time 1 variables to Time 2 variables, including a number of indirect effects on peer rejection (see Figure 6.1).

The relation between violent video game exposure and later aggression was strongest for physical aggression and weakest for relational aggression. This was largely expected, mainly because violent video games explicitly model and reinforce physical aggression. It also may be due partially to the manner in which video game violence was measured, by asking specifically about the violence in favorite video games, rather than about insulting or sarcastic content. Media exposure measures that focus on relational aggression displayed by television and video game characters might well uncover a stronger link to relational aggression by youths consuming such media. A pilot study has yielded such a link between relationally aggressive media exposure and relationally aggressive behavior (Bonacci, Tapscott, Carnagey, Wade, & Gentile, 2004).

Time 1 video game violence predicted Time 2 aggressive and prosocial behaviors, but the reverse was also found (Table 6.3). Although generally lower, Time 2 video game violence was significantly positively correlated with hostile attribution bias and verbal and physical aggression, and was negatively correlated with prosocial behavior at Time 1. The most plausible interpretation, as others have suggested (e.g., Donnerstein, Slaby, & Eron, 1994; Huesmann & Miller, 1994), is that there is a bidirectional relationship between media violence exposure and aggressive behaviors, at least in the short-term. It may be that over the long term (e.g., 11 years in Lefkowitz, Eron, Walder, & Huesmann, 1972), there is no relation between early aggressive behavior and later media violence exposure, but there is in the short-term (e.g., between 2 and 6 months in this study). Of course, there is no inherent contradiction between there being bidirectional longitudinal effects of media violence exposure and aggressive inclinations, of either equal or unequal magnitude. However, in the broader media violence literature, the evidence that early media violence exposure leads to later aggressive behavior is considerably stronger than evidence of early aggressiveness leading to later high levels of media violence exposure (Anderson et al., 2003). Whether this pattern is different for long-term longitudinal effects in the video game domain remains an open empirical question.

In sum, Study 3 lends considerable support to the theoretical proposition that repeated exposure to violent video games causes increases in the likelihood of future aggression. It did so directly; the correlation between Time 1 video game violence exposure and Time 2 aggression remained significant even after Time 1 aggression was statistically controlled. It also did so indirectly by finding considerable evidence that the long-term effect is at least partially due to changes in other theoretically based variables, such as the hostile attribution bias. Furthermore, the results contradicted several alternative explanations. As noted earlier, in scientific domains confidence in causal hypotheses is largely based on the convergence (triangulation) of results from different methods testing a causal theoretical model with empirical studies that could yield results that either support or contradict the model, and by testing (and ruling out) alternative explanations.

The more general media violence research domain reached the threshold for strong causal statements a number of years ago. In the recent past, such strong causal statements specifically addressed to violent video game effects relied in part on this more extensive (and certainly relevant) research literature. Now, however, strong causal statements for both long-term and short-term effects of violent video games can be made solely on the basis of research conducted on violent video games. The following sections further illustrate violent video game effects from the risk factor perspective.

7

Risk Factor Illustrations

Although all three studies found results consistent with theoretical predictions, the percentage of variance in aggressive behaviors uniquely explained by video game violence exposure was in the small to moderate range. As we have argued here and elsewhere (Anderson et al., 2003; Gentile & Sesma, 2003), from a developmental perspective it is useful to consider media violence within a developmental risks and resilience approach and to understand media violence as only one of the multiple risk factors that can cause increases in the likelihood of aggressive and violent behavior. In this section, we use the results of our three new studies to examine how various risk factors combine to predict increases in aggressive behaviors.

Violence Risk Factors for Children and College Students (Study 1)

The main purpose of Study 1 was to examine experimentally the effects of brief exposure to either a violent or a nonviolent video game on a standard laboratory measure of aggression. However, Study 1 also included measures of violent behavior, adult involvement in media habits, and habitual exposure to violent video games. This allows a rudimentary examination of these risk factors. The correlational and regression analyses (reported in an earlier section) on the violent behavior measure revealed significant main effects of video game violence exposure and adult involvement in media habits, as well as an exposure by involvement interaction. To further illustrate the effects of video game violence on violent behavior among this sample of elementary school and college students, we categorized participants on the basis of whether or not they reported having committed more than one act of violence (seventy-fifth percentile) in the previous year on the violent behavior measure. We then computed the best-fit model with habitual video game violence exposure, adult involvement, their interaction, and age as predictors of violent behavior, and used this predictive model to illustrate the risk factor effects.

Figure 7.1 illustrates the effects of low (fifth percentile), median, and high (ninety-fifth percentile) levels of video game violence exposure and adult involvement on likelihood of being involved in multiple violent acts in the past year. The figure shows the likelihood of violent acts as predicted by the regression equation with each of the predictors, which allows us to see how multiple risk factors stack up to increase the likelihood of aggressive behaviors. We do not report significance values again here, as they have already been reported earlier. However, each of the models demonstrated in this chapter are statistically significant, and we argue that the figures presented here demonstrate that the risk and protective factors are of practical significance as well. As Figure 7.1 shows, when adult involvement was high, video game violence had little impact on violence. But when it was low, playing a lot of violent video games was associated with a relatively high likelihood of multiple acts of violence. This demonstrates both that violent video game exposure is a risk factor for aggression and that parental involvement in children's media habits is a protective factor.

Violence Risk Factors for High School Students (Study 2)

The destructive testing and regression analyses on the high school students' data in Study 2 suggest that four variables be considered as somewhat independent risk factors for aggressive and violent behavior: exposure to violent video games, believing that aggression is normative, having a positive orientation to violence, and being a relatively unforgiving person. To further illustrate the effects of video game violence on violent behavior among high school students, we categorized participants on the basis of whether or not they reported having committed more than eight acts of violence (seventy-fifth percentile) in the previous year on the violent behavior measure. We then computed the best-fit model with these four risk factors as predictors of frequent violence, and used this model to illustrate the risk factor effects.

Figure 7.2 illustrates the effect of low (fifth percentile), median, and

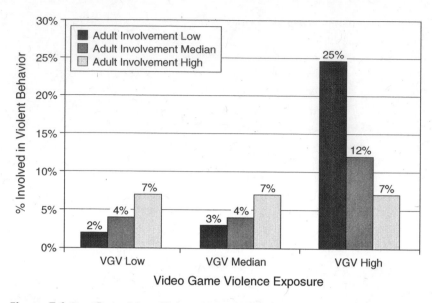

Figure 7.1 Best fit model predictions of percentage of elementary school and college students reporting multiple instances of violent behavior in the preceding year as a function of video game violence (VGV) and adult involvement in media habits.

high (ninety-fifth percentile) levels of video game violence exposure on likelihood of being frequently involved in violent acts, and does so when all of the other three predictors are at their low-risk levels, at their median, or at their high-risk levels (5%, 95%, for low and high risk, except forgiveness, for which the percentiles are reversed).

As can be seen, students with low-risk factor scores and low to moderate exposure to violent video games were very unlikely (0%) to engage in a high frequency of violent behavior. However, high exposure to violent video games increased the likelihood of frequent violent behavior to 15% even when the other risk factors were low.

Similar patterns emerged both when the other risk factors were at a moderate level (median) and when they were at a high level. In both cases, moderate exposure to violent video games was associated with a slight increase in likelihood of frequent violence. More important, high exposure to violent video games was associated with substantial increases in likelihood of frequent violent behavior. When the other risk factors were at a moderate level, the likelihood of frequent violent behavior almost tripled from low (15%) to high (43%) video game violence exposure, an increase in absolute terms of 28%. When the other risk factors were at a high level,

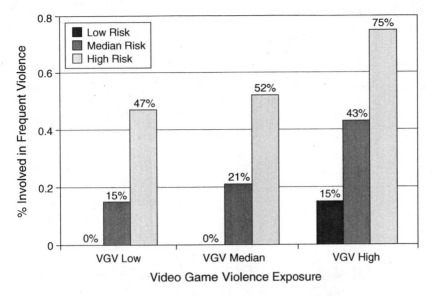

Figure 7.2 Best fit model predictions of percentage of high school students reporting high levels of violent behavior (more than 8 violent acts in the preceding year) as a function of video game violence (VGV) and level of risk of three additional risk factors (high positive orientation toward violence, high normative aggressive beliefs, low trait forgivingness).

the likelihood of frequent violent behavior increased from low (47%) to high (75%) video game violence exposure, an increase in absolute terms of 28%.

This figure also illustrates that the cumulative effect of the other three risk factors is quite large at all three levels of video game violence exposure. For example, among participants at the high end of the video game violence continuum, the likelihood of being involved in frequent violent behavior increased from 15% when other risk factors were low to 75% when they were high.

Figure 7.3 illustrates the relative impact of the four risk factors. Using the same best-fit regression model, we predicted the likelihood of frequent violent behavior for each risk factor (fifth and ninety-fifth percentiles) when the other three risk factors were at a median level. As can be seen in Figure 7.3, a positive orientation toward violence and high exposure to violent video games yielded considerably larger effects than did forgivingness and normative aggressive beliefs. However, even in the latter two cases the effects on involvement in frequent violence can be seen as substantial.

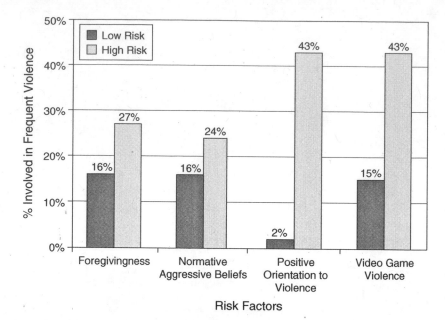

Figure 7.3 Best fit model predictions of percentage of high school students reporting high levels of violent behavior (more than 8 violent acts in the preceding year) as a function low- and high-risk levels of trait forgivingness, normative aggressive beliefs, positive orientation toward violence, and video game violence. Note: For each model, all other risk factors were set at the median.

More Violence Risk Factors for Children (Study 3)

Because of its longitudinal nature, Study 3 analyses of risk factors are truly predictive across time. We used data gathered at Time 1 to predict aggression at Time 2, again with a focus on the effects of exposure to violent video games. Figures 7.4, 7.5, and 7.6 display illustrations of this approach. Each bar represents the percentage of students predicted by the best-fit statistical model of the results to have been involved in a physical fight by Time 2 during the school year.

In Figure 7.4, the students are split by sex and by high, moderate, or low video game violence exposure at Time 1.[1] The high and low groups repre-

---

[1] To create these graphs, logistic regressions were conducted to predict physical fights at Time 2 with each list of independent variables. High, medium, and low values for each variable were created by using the ninety-fifth, fiftieth, and fifth percentile scores on each variable, and inserting them into the equation $p = e^x/(1+e^x)$, where p is the probability of a fight at Time 2 and x is the result from inserting the high, medium, and low values into the logistic equation $x = B_{constant} + B_{sex}(\text{value}) + B_{mve}(\text{value})$. If interaction terms were nonsignificant, they were not included in the equation.

sent the ninety-fifth and fifth percentile scores, respectively. The moderate group represents scoring at the median value. As can be seen in Figure 7.4, both variables matter—females who are low in video game violence at Time 1 are the least likely to have been involved in physical fights at Time 2; in contrast, males who are high in video game violence at Time 1 are the most likely to have been involved in physical fights at Time 2.

In Figure 7.5, the students are split by high or low hostile attribution bias at Time 1 and by high, moderate, or low violent game exposure at Time 1. Again, both variables matter—overall, children with a hostile attribution bias are more likely to be involved in physical fights, but students who play the most violent games are more likely to be involved in fights regardless of whether they have a hostile attribution bias. As each additional risk factor increases, the risk of physical aggression increases. If a child is high on both Time 1 hostile attribution bias and video game violence exposure, there is a 79% likelihood that that child will get into a physical fight by Time 2.

Similarly in Figure 7.6, the students are split by whether they had reported being involved in physical fights at Time 1 and by high or low video game violence at Time 1. Again, both variables matter—the students who had not been in fights at Time 1 and who were low on video game violence at Time 1 are the least likely to have been involved in physical

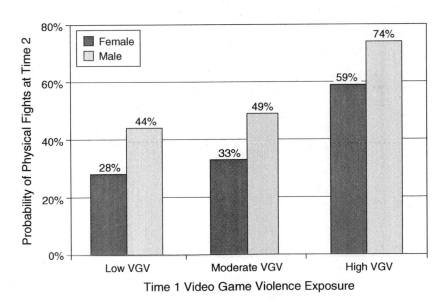

Figure 7.4 Predicted likelihood of physical fights at Time 2 as a function of sex and video game violence exposure.

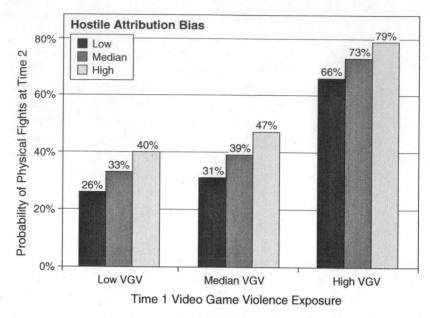

Figure 7.5 Predicted likelihood of physical fights at Time 2 as a function of hostile attribution bias and video game violence exposure.

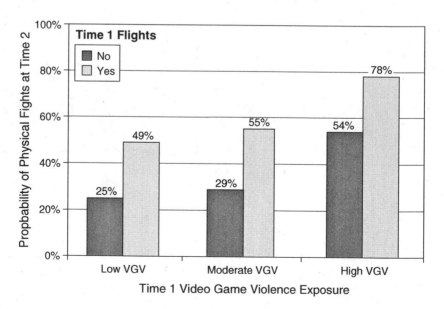

Figure 7.6 Predicted likelihood of physical fights at Time 2 as a function of involvement in physical fights and video game violence exposure at Time 1.

fights at Time 2; in contrast, the students who had been involved in physical fights at Time 1 and also were high on video game violence at Time 1 are the most likely to have been involved in physical fights at Time 2.

As these three figures show, no one variable is the sole or primary cause of aggression. Yet, each of these variables, hostile attribution bias, sex, video game violence exposure, and prior aggressive behavior is related to future aggressive behavior. As such, each is appropriately described as a risk factor for aggression. One strength of this approach is that it predicts the results shown in Figures 7.4, 7.5, and 7.6, namely that as risk factors combine, the risk of aggressive behavior increases. A media diet high in violence in combination with other risk factors produces an effect greater than either risk factor alone. In fact, one should notice that if a student is in the high video game violence group he or she is very likely to get into fights at Time 2, even if he or she is at low risk on the other variable. Thus, the girls who play a lot of violent video games are *more* likely than boys who play the median amount to get into fights. Similarly, students who are low on hostile attribution bias but play a lot of violent video games are more likely to get into fights than students who are high on hostile attribution bias who do not play violent video games. This pattern is also similar for children who have not been involved in fights at Time 1 but who play a lot of violent video games.

Using this risk-factor approach, we could also predict that if we combined more risk factors, the ability to predict fights should get stronger and more fine-grained. Figure 7.7 displays the predicted likelihood of physical fights at Time 2 based on four risk factors: whether children score high or low on hostile attribution bias, whether children are male or female, whether children had been involved in physical fights at Time 1, and whether children consume a low or high amount of video game violence. As can be seen, all four variables matter: children with high hostile attribution bias are more likely to get into fights; prior fighting predicts later fighting; boys are more likely to get into fights; and high video game violence exposure predicts greater likelihood of fights. As predicted by the risk-factor approach, the group with the least predicted risk of physical fights is (1) girls who have (2) a low hostile attribution bias, (3) have not been involved in fights previously, and (4) who do not play violent video games. The group with the greatest predicted risk of physical fights is (1) boys who have (2) a high hostile attribution bias, (3) have been involved in fights previously, and (4) who play a lot of violent video games.

This pattern is identical to that found in a study of adolescents, where violent video game play and trait hostility were both measured (Gentile et al., 2004). Both hostility and violent game play were related to physical fights, but the combination was greater than either alone.

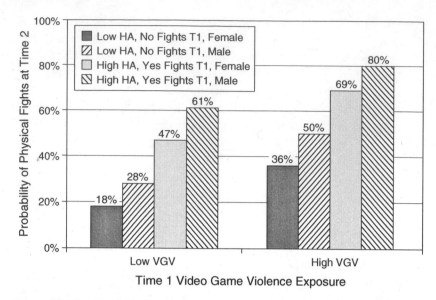

Figure 7.7 Predicted likelihood of physical fights at Time 2 as a function of hostile attribution bias, involvement in physical fights at Time 1, sex, and video game violence exposure.

Additional confirmation of the utility of the risk-factor approach would be to examine the effects of protective factors. Theoretically, and as seen in Study 1, active parental involvement in children's media habits should serve as a protective factor for later aggressive habits (Austin, 1993, Dorr & Rabin, 1995; Lin & Atkin, 1989). As can be seen in Figure 7.8, this hypothesis is borne out by the data. Although children who are exposed to greater amounts of video game violence at Time 1 are more likely to be involved in physical fights by Time 2, if their parents are more involved in their media habits then their risk of fights is decreased. As would be predicted, the greatest likelihood of fights at Time 2 is predicted by high video game violence exposure and low parental involvement (82% likelihood). Conversely, the lowest likelihood of fights is predicted by low video game violence exposure and high parental involvement (27%).

Figure 7.9 displays the results of the logistic equation predicting Time 2 fights from the combination of hostile attribution bias, involvement in physical fights at Time 1, sex, video game violence exposure, and parental involvement. Not all combinations are shown, but as predicted by the risk and protective factor approach, the group with the least predicted risk of physical fights (16%) are (1) girls who have (2) a low hostile attribution bias, (3) have not been involved in fights previously, (4) who do not play violent video games, and (5) who have parents who are highly involved in

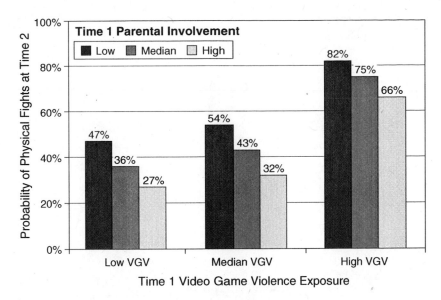

Figure 7.8 Predicted likelihood of physical fights at Time 2 as a function of Time 1 parental involvement and video game violence exposure.

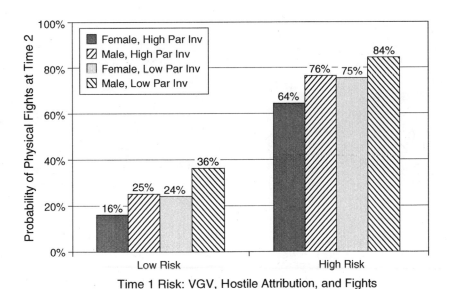

Figure 7.9 Predicted likelihood of physical fights at Time 2 as a function of hostile attribution bias, video game violence exposure, physical fights at Time 1, sex, and parental involvement.

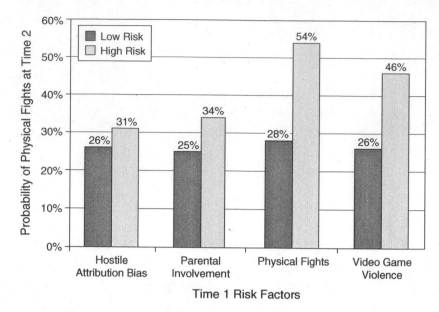

Figure 7.10 Best fit model predictions of the probability of elementary school students engaging in physical fights at Time 2 as a function Time 1 low- and high-risk levels of hostile attribution bias, parental involvement in media, physical fights, and video game violence. Note: For each model, all other risk factors were set at the median.

their media habits. Children with the greatest predicted risk of physical fights (84%) are (1) boys who have (2) a high hostile attribution bias, (3) have been involved in fights previously, (4) who spend a lot of time playing violent video games, and (5) whose parents are not involved in their media habits.

Figure 7.10 illustrates the relative impact of four risk and protective factors. Using the same best-fit regression model, we predicted the likelihood of physical fights for each risk factor (fifth and ninety-fifth percentiles) when the other three risk factors were at a median level. As can be seen in Figure 7.10, prior fights and high exposure to violent video games almost double the risk of future fights, and both yielded considerably larger effects than did hostile attribution bias and parental involvement in children's media habits. However, even in the latter two cases the effects on involvement in physical fights can be seen as substantial.

PART III

GENERAL DISCUSSION (WHAT DOES IT ALL MEAN?)

In Part III we summarize and discuss our new findings and their implications for several key issues. Chapter 8 focuses on the new findings and how they relate to a host of theoretical issues. Chapter 9 discusses the magnitude of media violence effects, catharsis (venting) ideas that abound in popular culture, and a host of public policy questions. Chapter 10 offers a brief summary of implications for parents and for future public policy debates in this area.

8

New Findings and Their Implications

The three studies reported in this monograph yielded a host of new findings. Most concern the effects of exposure to violent video games on aggressive behavior, though a few other findings are also of special interest. Many of the main new findings can be broken down by type of research method.

Experimental

There were three main experimental findings from Study 1. First, children's video games with violent content increased aggressive behavior in the laboratory. This experimental effect occurred with males and females, with children and college students, with individuals with high and low media violence exposure, with participants who had and did not have television or video game media available in their bedrooms, and with individuals with high and low media violence preference. Second, the violent children's games produced an increase in aggression at least as large at the T-rated video games; indeed, the children's violent game increase was slightly (nonsignificantly) larger. Combined, these first two main experimental findings contradict two basic assumptions made by parents, the video game industry, and various public policy groups: (1) that children's games are safe for all ages even if they have aggressive content, and (2) that T-rated violent games have a significantly bigger immediate negative impact on players than violent children's games. Some caution is needed in interpreting these latter findings, in part because only two violent children's games and two violent T-rated games were compared, in part because extraordinary findings require extraordinary evidence (including replication), and in part because the children's violent and T-violent game difference in aggression was not statistically significant. It is possible that other selections of children's and T-rated violent games would yield slightly different results. In fact, our expectation is that with truly huge sample sizes and large numbers of violent children's and T-rated games, their respective effects on short-term aggression in the lab will prove to be either about the same (as in the current results) or that the T-rated games might have a slightly greater aggression-enhancing effect. In any case, the main point brought home by the present findings is that children's video games with violent content increase aggression, and do so with a magnitude that is comparable to T-rated violent games.

The third experimental finding was that participants rated the T-rated violent games as containing more violence than the violent children's games. This confirmed our hunch that such violence ratings by normal game-playing individuals (as well as the Entertainment Software Rating Board) are more heavily influenced by the amount of blood and gore and perhaps the realism of the game characters (versus cute cartoon-like characters, happy music, and sound effects) than by the body count or the actual frequency and degree of harm of the game actions (Potter, 1999).

Cross-Section Correlational

Many important cross-sectional correlational findings emerged from all three studies. In our view, five findings are especially important and novel. First, level of exposure to video game violence was quite strongly related to a wide array of forms of aggression (e.g., verbal, moderate physical, violent), a wide range of ages of research participants (elementary school, high school, and young adults), and across many different measures of aggressive and violent behavior. For example, in Study 2, with high school students, the correlation with violent behavior was $r = 0.35$, and with moderate physical aggression was $r = 0.46$. Second, video game violence exposure was positively related to a host of aggression-related variables such as trait anger and hostility, attitudes toward violence, and hostile attribution bias. Third, the amount of screen time (i.e., time spent playing video games and watching television and films per week) was more strongly associated with school performance than was video game violence exposure. Fourth, video game violence was a significant risk factor for aggression and violence even when other important risk factors were statistically controlled. Fifth, trait forgivingness was strongly negatively associated with aggression in Study 2.

Longitudinal

Because there are no previously published studies of the longitudinal effects of playing violent video games, the present findings are especially unique. By far the most important finding was the longitudinal change in physical aggression attributed directly to repeated exposure to violent video games (e.g., Figures 6.1 and 6.2). A second key finding was the mediated effect of video game violence on aggression via hostile attribution bias. A third key finding was the negative effect of video game violence on prosocial behavior. It appears that not only does repeated exposure to violent video games increase aggressive behavior, but it also decreases empathic helpful behavior. A fourth finding of especial interest was the direct effect of total screen time on decline in school performance.

Old Versus New Violent Media

A frequent question concerns the relative size of the effects of older forms of media violence (e.g., television, films) compared to newer and more interactive forms such as violent video games. Are violent video games more harmful than violent television shows or films? This seemingly simple question cloaks a host of complex conceptual and methodological issues. For example, does the questioner mean amount of harm per hour of exposure, or total amount of harm regardless of relative exposures? What time frame—short term or long term? What type of harm—aggressive behavior, thoughts, and feelings; desensitization to scenes or thoughts of violence; addiction to the medium?

Even once a more specific question has been posed, a host of difficulties remain. For example, consider the following question: Does brief exposure to a violent video game produce a bigger increase in short-term aggressive behavior than an equivalent exposure to a violent TV episode? This question clearly suggests an experimental design, one that could be conducted in either field (e.g., after-school program) or laboratory (e.g., university lab) settings. Obviously, one would need (at minimum) a violent video game condition and a violent TV episode condition. But how does the researcher equate these two conditions on other factors? What factors *should* be equated? Amount of time? (Probably yes.) Interest level? (Probably yes.) Amount of violence? (Maybe not, because one key difference between the genres is that violent video games typically involve many more violent acts per hour than violent television shows.) What about control conditions? Should we have both a nonviolent video game and a nonviolent television show?

Theoretically, it is not even clear that one should expect to see a difference between old versus new forms of media violence effects in a short-term context, where most of the immediate effects are likely the result of some type of priming process (e.g., Anderson et al., 2003). However, there are several reasons to expect that given equivalent amounts of exposure over time, violent video games are likely to produce larger negative long-term effects on physical aggression and several other aggression-related variables than violent television and films (e.g., Anderson & Dill, 2000; Dill & Dill, 1998; Gentile & Anderson, 2003). Most of these reasons revolve around the interactive nature of video games, their excellence as teaching and learning tools, and the direct rewards of choosing violence (Gentile & Gentile, under review).

The long-term perspective is also fraught with methodological and conceptual pitfalls but does suggest examining cross-sectional and longitudinal comparisons between new versus old forms of media violence. There have been few attempts to make such comparisons. One way to do so is to compare the average effect size of violent video games to the average of violent television and film effects (e.g., Sherry, 2001). Though comparisons of meta-analytically derived effect sizes can be useful in making gross comparisons across very different domains of research (such as the relative effect sizes of second hand smoke on cancer versus television violence on aggression, e.g., Bushman & Huesmann, 2001), such comparisons are less useful when trying to make fine distinctions between closely related domains such as the old versus new media violence question. Different subject populations, methodologies, eras, quality of original empirical studies, and outcome variables all contribute to the danger of such comparisons.

A better approach is to compare the effects of old versus new forms of media violence within the same cross-sectional or longitudinal study. Such an approach does not by any means solve all of the conceptual and methodological issues, but it is certainly more informative. One of the first studies (maybe the first) to report relevant findings of this type was by Funk, Baldacci, Pasold, and Baumgardner (2004). In a correlational study, they found greater effects of violent video games than of television on empathy and attitudes.

Each of the present three studies also allowed comparative tests of the relative effects of violent video game exposure versus violent television and film exposure on aggressive behavior. In Study 1, self-reported violent behavior was more strongly and uniquely associated with video game violence exposure than with television and movie violence exposure. Study 2 also found that video game violence exposure was more strongly and uniquely associated with violent behavior and physical aggression than television and film violence exposure. Finally, Study 3 found that video game violence was more uniquely associated with increases in physical aggression over time, whereas TV and film violence appeared to be slightly more uniquely associated with increases in verbal aggression over time. This latter finding is consistent with differences in the violence content between video games (very little verbal aggression) and television and films (considerable verbal aggression).

Vulnerability, Risk, and Resilience

The recent review of the entire media violence domain (Anderson et al., 2003) concluded that although there was some evidence of moderating variables and differential risk and vulnerabilities, the overall strength of that evidence was considerably weaker than the evidence for fairly general and robust negative effects of exposure to media violence. Indeed, there is no convincing evidence in the extant literature that any particular group of people (by age, sex, personality disposition or trait, economic circumstances, family characteristics, or race) is wholly immune to the aggression-enhancing effects of media violence. The present studies further bolster this finding. Although there were dozens of opportunities for interactions involving potential moderator effects to emerge in these three studies, only two were statistically significant. One should expect several such "significant" interactions merely by chance, so it is best to avoid being overconfident that the two that did emerge were not due to statistical chance. In Study 1, there was evidence that parental involvement in youths' media usage might reduce the short-term effect of playing a violent children's game on aggressive behavior in that laboratory situation. In Study 2, there was evidence that highly forgiving individuals might be somewhat less negatively affected by video game violence than low forgiving people; however, this latter effect occurred only for the violence measure, but not for the verbal or moderate physical aggression measures in that study. Thus, based on current and prior evidence, it appears that no group or individual can be considered automatically immune to the aggression-enhancing effects of repeated exposure to media violence or to video game violence. Conversely, it also appears that no group or individual can be considered automatically more vulnerable to the effects of media violence exposure. This point has recently also been made by other developmental aggression theorists (e.g., Dodge & Petit, 2003) that it is "one thing to posit interactive models but quite another to find evidence consistent with them" (Petit, 2004, p. 196). However, we too believe that there is sufficient evidence of potential moderating effects and sufficient complexity in this domain (e.g., long-term versus short-term effects on physical versus verbal aggression) to warrant additional research.

Although the evidence for immunity and vulnerability differences is weak overall, the evidence for a different form of risk and resilience model appears much stronger. The present studies suggest that media violence is a risk factor that essentially adds to the effects of other known risk factors for aggressive and violent behavior. No single risk factor dominates an individual's overall risk for behaving violently in the future, but the presence of multiple risk factors (including habitual exposure to media violence) and the absence of resilience factors add up to a fairly accurate probabilistic prediction of future aggressive behavior (e.g., Figure 7.9). To a great extent, this additive risk and resilience model explains the paradox we all face when the ubiquitous 14-year-old points out that he has played violent video games for nine years and still has not killed any real people.

Triangulation, Media Violence, and the General Aggression Model

The General Aggression Model nicely integrates the findings from the present studies as well as prior research on media violence and on human aggression in general. The picture of human aggression that emerges from the General Aggression Model is one of a holistic learning system influenced by biological, cultural, sociological, familial, and individual factors that prepare the person to perceive and respond to ongoing social interactions in a variety of complex ways. Some factors combine, over time and repeated experience, to produce individuals who are relatively more prepared to perceive threats (sometimes when they don't exist) and to respond to them with forceful physical aggression. Such individuals become habitually aggressive people, especially if they are in environments in which potentially provocative situations arise with some frequency.

Habitual exposure to media violence is one factor (and only one of many) that contributes to the development of aggressive individuals, and possibly to aggressive cultures. The triangulation approach in the conduct of modern science is especially useful in such complex theoretical domains as human aggression. The three studies reported in the present monograph used each of the three main research designs (experimental, cross-sectional, longitudinal), multiple research populations, and multiple measures of aggression and of aggression-related variables. The consistent findings in support of the hypothesis that exposure to video game violence can increase aggression, and the consistent findings that alternative explanations of these results do not hold up under empirical scrutiny, strongly support the General Aggression Model's developmental hypotheses about human aggression in general and its interpretation of how media violence affects those exposed to it.

Furthermore, the consistent findings emerging from multiple research groups using multiple research designs, target populations, and research methods further support our developmental version of the General Aggression Model and of media violence effects. Triangulation works here at an even broader level. Specifically, most of the General Aggression Model, and of related media violence theoretical models, is based on empirically based findings throughout psychology that have no direct ties to human aggression. For instance, basic research on the development and automatization of perceptual knowledge structures underlies and supports theorizing about the development of aggressive knowledge structures. Similarly, basic research in multiple domains as varied as cognitive neuroscience, social psychology, developmental psychology, personality psychology, biological psychology, and abnormal psychology plays a role in defining the basic tenets of any general model of human behavior, including the General Aggression Model. Critics, both the well-meaning scientific colleagues as well as the less-well meaning fiscally motivated ones, often miss this very valuable point: the theoretical and empirical foundation of media violence work is incredibly broad and deep. At this point in the history of media violence research, the triangulation approach to examining the basic research and theories of how repeatedly playing violent video games (or watching violent television shows) can cause a probabilistic increase in the likelihood of that person behaving in a very aggressive manner at a later time has yielded overwhelming evidence. To be sure, there are a number of research questions in need of additional testing. For one example, longer-term longitudinal studies of video game violence effects are clearly needed. Another example is the need for additional studies to tease apart media violence factors that might have a relatively bigger effect on short-term aggression (priming factors?) versus those that have a relatively bigger effect on long-term aggression (desensitization factors?). But the basic media violence phenomena are well understood, and that understanding (in our view) derives from theory, data testing that theory, and a broad triangulation approach to evaluating, revising, and further testing of basic theory.

Developmental Theory Implications

Although many of the implications of these three studies are fairly obvious, we believe it important to note several of particular relevance to developmental theories. First and foremost, many "third variable" theories (i.e., those that maintain all violent video game effects on children and adolescents are mere accidents of confounded variables) are strongly contradicted by the results of all three studies. The experimental findings of Study 1 rule out such third variable alternative explanations by virtue of the experimental research method itself; the control variables used in that study further contradict several third variable alternatives. The cross-sectional and longitudinal results also provide convergent evidence in support of a causal model of violent video game effects, and virtually no evidence that several frequently hypothesized "confounded" third variables account for any sizable portion of the obtained effects.

Second, developmental theories that hypothesize a large age vulnerability effect due to lower ability to distinguish reality from fantasy also were strongly contradicted by the results. A more parsimonious model emphasizing the importance of priming, social learning, and social cognitive effects fits the data much better.

Third, a risk and resilience model that is largely additive (rather than interactive) fit the overall patterns of data quite well. Older risk and resilience models that assume the existence of immune groups or individuals, and thereby predict statistical interactions between violent video game exposure and resilient characteristics, did not fare well. This does not refute the possibility of interactive models. Dodge and Petit (2003) provide evidence for both additive models and interactive models in the development of aggressive conduct problems, including interactions with sex and age (which we did not find).

Regardless of whether certain risk and resilience factors moderate the effects of violent video game exposure, the developmental story told by these data is the same. As with other risk and resilience models, our model proposes that certain early contexts would put children at probabilistic risk for later aggression. These early contexts include, but are not limited to, biological factors (e.g., sex), sociocultural factors at several ecological levels (e.g., witnessing violence in the family or neighborhood), parenting practices (e.g., harsh discipline, parental monitoring), peer influences (e.g., aggressive peers, peer rejection, etc.), and exposure to media violence. We have proposed that exposure to violent video games is likely to result in rehearsal and learning of aggressive scripts, aggressive beliefs, and aggressive expectation schemata (e.g., hostile attribution bias). These changes in turn lead to increases in aggressive personality and behaviors and decreases in prosocial behavior. These behavioral changes can then lead to changes in the social environment, such as peer rejection. The three studies reported here provide evidence for this developmental sequence. However, the developmental story is likely to continue beyond what was studied here. Once rejected by the dominant peer group, these aggressive children are likely to form cliques with other aggressive children. In that subculture, the children will also be likely to reinforce each other's aggressive attitudes, behaviors, and media habits. Thus a vicious circle is provided with additional spin.

The risk-factor approach advocated here also allows developmental theory to better address the common question of whether the beginning of the media violence → aggression → media violence → aggression cycle is due to aggressive children preferring to play violent video games or due to violent video games making children more aggressive. Regardless of the *initial cause*, violent video games are clearly not going to reduce children's aggressive tendencies. From the evidence presented in this monograph, it appears that no matter how many risk and protective factors the child already has, playing violent video games still adds *additional risk* for future increased aggressive behavior.

9

Interpretations and Public Policy

Effect Size

Although most social scientists recognize that there is an empirically demonstrated effect of media violence exposure on aggression, many scientists mistakenly believe that the size of the effect is trivially small. There probably are several reasons for this belief. Perhaps the most typical is statistical in nature. We were all taught in introductory statistics classes to square a correlation coefficient in order to determine how much variance can be accounted for. Thus, an effect size of 0.20 (in r terms) accounts for only 4% of the variance. Effects sizes in the 0.20 range are common in media violence studies. Many people may feel that this is not a large percentage of variance, and in absolute terms they may be right. Yet human aggression is a multicausal phenomenon. Why someone acts aggressively in a given situation is influenced by hundreds of factors, some proximal and some distal, some personal and some situational. If it is true that there are hundreds of variables that have some influence on whether an individual acts aggressively, then we should not expect any single variable to account for even *1%* of the variance in aggression. Therefore, if any one variable can account for 1% or more of the variance, then that variable does not seem to us to be trivial. Indeed, among many empirically identified risk factors for aggression, media violence exposure accounts for at least as much variance as most others. Table 9.1 lists a number of factors that have been identified as risk factors for youth violence and aggression, as well as estimates of the magnitude of their longitudinal effect sizes. As shown in Table 9.1, most risk factors that many aggression scholars would call "important" do not account for a great deal of variance individually (e.g., being male accounts for 3.6%, having a low IQ accounts for 1.2%, and having abusive parents accounts for 0.8%). These effect sizes are generally lower than those found in meta-analyses of media violence studies (e.g., Anderson & Bushman, 2001; Bushman & Anderson, 2001; Comstock & Scharrer, 2003; Paik & Comstock, 1994). Therefore, on an empirical basis alone, the effects of media violence exposure generally and violent video game exposure in particular are not trivial. Furthermore, as shown in Table 9.1 longitudinal effects of media violence in general and of the one true longitudinal violent video game study are larger than many other known risk factors. Indeed, in our Study 3, violent video game exposure at Time 1 accounted for more variance in aggression at Time 2 (8.8% after controlling for sex) than any other factor listed in Table 9.1 except gang membership (9.6%). Although the estimated effect size for violent video games is likely to change somewhat (perhaps becoming larger, or smaller) as additional longitudinal studies are completed, it is clear that the effect is likely to remain a very important one.

Furthermore, when one considers this issue from an epidemiological perspective, the amount of the effect is clearly not trivial. There are approximately 50 million children in the United States. Almost all children play video games (Gentile & Walsh, 2002). If society reduced the amount

TABLE 9.1   Longitudinal effect sizes of several empirically identified long-term risk factors for aggressive/ and violent behavior

Risk Factor	Effect Size	Variance Accounted for (%)
Gang membership	.31	9.6%
Video Game Violence*	**.30**	**8.8%**
Psychological condition	.19	3.6%
Poor parent-child relations	.19	3.6%
Being male	.19	3.6%
Prior physical violence	.18	3.2%
Media Violence**	**.17**	**2.9%**
Antisocial parents	.16	2.6%
Low IQ	.11	1.2%
Broken home	.10	1.0%
Poverty	.10	1.0%
Risk-taking	.09	0.8%
Abusive parents	.09	0.8%
Substance use	.06	0.4%

Adapted from U.S. Department of Health and Human Services. (2001). *Youth Violence: A Report of the Surgeon General.* Rockville, MD: U.S. Government Printing Office. *From Study 3, with sex statistically controlled. **From Anderson and Bushman, 2002c.

of exposure children have to violent video games and other violent media, there would probably be a tremendous societal impact. In fact, if we just reduced the exposure for 1% of the children, theoretically that would reduce aggression for 500,000 children.

There have been several excellent explorations of why and under what conditions "small" effect sizes actually yield large effects. When the effects accumulate across time, when large portions of the population are exposed to the risk factor, and when the consequences are severe, statistically small effects become much larger in both a statistical and a practical sense (e.g., Abelson, 1985; Rosenthal, 1986, 1990). Furthermore, the magnitude of media violence effect sizes, particularly the video game violence effect sizes found in the present studies, are considerably larger than many effect sizes deemed large in medical and other social contexts (Bushman & Huesmann, 2001). For example, media violence effects are larger than the effects of passive smoke on lung cancer (Wells, 1998), exposure to lead and IQ scores in children (Needleman and Gatsonis, 1990), nicotine patches and smoking cessation (Fiore, Smith, Jorenby, and Baker, 1994), calcium intake and bone mass (Welten, Kemper, Post, and van Staveren, 1995), and exposure to asbestos and laryngeal cancer (Smith, Handley, and Wood, 1990).

Finally, as we demonstrated in the risk factor figures (Figures 7.1–7.10), the modest percent-of-variance-explained results actually translated into substantial differences in aggression and violence rates. This was true in all three studies, for different ages, for boys and girls, and for serious forms of aggression.

Catharsis

Although the empirical evidence described here, and in hundreds of other studies, documents that exposure to violent video games and other forms of media violence in general lead to increased aggressive thoughts, feelings, and behaviors, there is still a common belief that playing violent video games or watching violent TV and films allows people to "vent" their aggression and therefore behave less aggressively after playing or watching. This concept of catharsis has a long history, and will be reviewed only briefly here. *Catharsis* was first described by Aristotle and was adapted by Freud for use in modern psychology.

One of Freud's reactions to World War I was to question how such horrors could come to pass. He reasoned that humans must have an instinctual aggression drive, which he titled "Thanatos." In his conception, Thanatos was a drive toward self-destruction, constantly in struggle with "Eros," a drive toward life. If Thanatos were to win this struggle, we would all kill ourselves. However, Freud posited two ways in which Thanatos could be released without suicide: displacement and catharsis. In this conception, displacement serves to help explain why we aggress toward others. We displace, or redirect, our aggressive energies toward others rather than ourselves. Furthermore, according to Freud, watching violence or engaging in mild displays of anger acts as catharsis—it allows us to vent some of the accumulated aggressive energy, leaving us emotionally calmed (Campbell, 1993). With regard to media violence, the catharsis hypothesis has been and continues to be popular, despite at least four critical flaws.

Flaw 1: Aggression Is Not a Drive

If Freud's concept of aggression being a drive were correct, then aggression can be conceptualized by a hydraulic metaphor. The pressure to aggress builds and builds over time, as a part of living, until it must be released, either by aggressing against the self or others. Yet when one compares aggression to other true drives, such as eating, drinking, and sleeping, it becomes evident that aggression is not similar. With a true drive, pressure builds to engage in an activity, and when we engage in that activity the pressure is reduced (for a time). If we do not eat, we get hungrier and hungrier, and if we still do not eat, we die. If we do not drink, we get thirstier and thirstier, and if we still do not drink, we die. The same goes for sleep and breathing. In contrast, if we do not behave aggressively, we do not get more aggressive, nor do we die for lack of aggression. Therefore, if aggression is not a drive, then catharsis is not needed. If, as we believe, aggression results from a combination of learned, biological, and situational factors, the concept of catharsis does little to add to an understanding of the development of aggression.

Flaw 2: Even If Catharsis Could Work, Modern Media Do It Incorrectly

The idea of catharsis as a "venting" of a drive isn't what the term meant when it was initially applied to media. The term *catharsis* was introduced by Aristotle, who believed that poetry (which at that time meant all media, including plays, music, and speeches) had powerful emotional effects.

In the *Poetics*, he defined tragedy in plays and poetry as "the imitation of an action that is serious and also, as having magnitude, complete in itself . . . in a dramatic, not a narrative form; with incidents arousing pity and fear, wherewith to accomplish its catharsis of such emotions" (*Poetics*, 1459b, 25–28). Thus, catharsis is the end part of tragedy. However, achieving catharsis required very specific ways of telling the story. Three are described below.

    1. The plot must be constructed very carefully.

> The Plot must be not simple but complex; and further, that it must imitate actions arousing fear and pity. . . . It follows, therefore, that there are three forms of Plot to be avoided. (1) A good man must not be seen passing from happiness to misery, or (2) a bad man from misery to happiness. The first situation is not fear-inspiring or piteous, but simply odious to us. The second is the most untragic that can be; it has no one of the requisites of Tragedy; it does not appeal to the human feeling in us, or to our pity, or to our fears. Nor, on the other hand, should (3) an extremely bad man be seen falling from happiness into misery. Such a story may arouse the human feeling in us, but it will not move us to either pity or fear; pity is occasioned by undeserved misfortune, and fear by that of one like ourselves. . . . There remains, then, the intermediate kind of personage, a man not preeminently virtuous and just, whose misfortune, however, is brought upon him not by vice and depravity but by some error of judgment. . . . The perfect Plot, accordingly, must have . . . the change in the hero's fortunes . . . from happiness to misery; and the cause of it must not lie in any depravity, but in some great error on his part. (*Poetics*, 1452b 30–1453a 16).

    2. For catharsis to occur, two critical emotions, *fear* and *pity*, both must be aroused. These can be aroused by either Plot or Spectacle (e.g., special effects). More important, however, is how the "tragic pleasure" of fear and pity are aroused. The conflict should arise *between friends* (rather than enemies or combatants) for it to be truly tragic and arouse the proper emotions. Aristotle notes that if the plot is not constructed thus, it gets the wrong emotional responses, such as shock and revulsion (Janko, 1987).

    3. The characters must be of a certain type. To arouse fear and pity, the characters must be noble, good, appropriate, realistic, and consistent.

    If we view current entertainment media, especially media violence, through this lens, we will see that the argument for catharsis of aggressive feelings does not hold. Aristotle repeatedly notes that catharsis requires feelings of fear and pity. If we think about action and adventure films, while there is much Spectacle, there is usually no pity aroused. The "bad guy" does something bad, the "good guy" fights with him, and ultimately wins. We do not pity either character, although we may feel fear and shock or pleasure at justice being served. Second, fear and pity must be aroused by an undeserved misfortune to the hero, through error and not through intention or depravity. This means that any pity felt for the "good guy" having something bad happen to him because of the "bad guy's" intention is not what Aristotle says works. Ultimately, it is unclear that Aristotle ever suggested catharsis could occur for viewers (rather than merely being a literary term), but even if he did, most modern media violence does not follow the correct Plots nor does it engage the correct emotions to achieve catharsis.

Flaw 3: Dearth of Supportive and Glut of Contradictory Empirical Evidence

The third critical flaw with the catharsis hypothesis is that there is almost no scientific evidence supporting it, whereas there is a great deal of scientific evidence for the opposite hypothesis. There have been hundreds of studies of media violence—most of which could be interpreted as studies of catharsis. For example, in the studies reported here, children could have had lower aggressive thoughts and behaviors after playing the violent video games. However, they did not. This pattern is also found in most other studies of media violence and aggressive behavior (e.g., Anderson et al., 2003). Therefore, hundreds of studies demonstrate that people become more aggressive after consuming media violence, not less.

In addition to studies of media violence, there have been several studies specifically designed to test whether aggressive behavior reduces or increases later aggression. In their seminal review of the catharsis hypothesis, Geen & Quanty (1977) demonstrated that, at best, aggression might produce decreased physiological arousal under specific conditions. But they also found that even when physiological arousal decreased after initial aggression, later aggressive behavior did not. Although there have been a handful of studies that suggest behavioral catharsis may occur, these studies have had methodological problems and are open to other interpretations. When the studies have been replicated with appropriate controls, the results tend to be the opposite—that aggressive behavior leads to increased aggressive behavior. After reviewing all the evidence, they stated, "therefore, we must conclude that the notion of catharsis has not been confirmed" (p. 33).

Over 20 years later, Geen (2001) summarized the catharsis literature in several areas: symbolic catharsis, such as viewing violence in the media or viewing aggressive sports; fantasizing about aggression; aggressing against inanimate objects; and aggressing against the antagonist. In every case, the weight of empirical evidence is against the theory of behavioral catharsis. That is, viewing, thinking about, or performing aggressive acts tends to increase later aggressive behavior, not reduce it. More recent studies on this topic further confirm these findings (e.g., Bushman, 2002; Bushman, Baumeister, & Stack, 1999).

Flaw 4: The Brain Is What the Brain Does

Although there is not space for a detailed description of neural network development, it is clear from what we know about the brain that behavioral catharsis of aggression is extremely unlikely. Learning is the process of making certain neural pathways work more readily than they did before. The technical term is long-term potentiation (LTP), in which a neuron that is stimulated repeatedly becomes more likely to fire because of that stimulation; that is, learning at the neural level is caused by repetition.

This makes a great deal of intuitive sense when we consider how most people remember telephone numbers. We repeat them. After repeating them several times, we no longer need to repeat them—we have learned them. This is how the brain works—the neurons that fire together, wire together. If catharsis were true, repeating the telephone number should make us *less* likely to remember and use it in the future. But in fact, repeating experiences is one of the most effective ways to learn something. Practice does make perfect (or at least more likely). Therefore, if one plays a violent video game in which one practices aggressive thoughts, feelings, and responses, it cannot lead to lowered aggressive thoughts, feelings, or responses over the long term. Even Aristotle knew this, as he believed that we become good by practicing being good.

Summary

It seems clear from this analysis that catharsis of aggressive behavior is not a valid phenomenon, neither conceptually nor empirically. Aggression is not a drive that must be vented. Even if Aristotle were right, modern media violence is not constructed in a way to achieve catharsis. In the hundreds of studies of media violence, catharsis has not been shown to work—rather the opposite has been demonstrated. Finally, given the way that the brain works, catharsis does not make sense. We do not become less likely to learn something by practicing it.

Given the lack of evidence for catharsis and the considerable weight of evidence against it, it may be surprising that it is still such a popular concept. Perhaps a clue to this is given by Bushman, Baumeister, & Stack (1999). When angered, behaving aggressively feels pleasurable. This may be misinterpreted by people to suggest that they would behave less aggressively in the future, when in fact aggressive behavior is more likely (perhaps partly because we believe we will feel better afterward). This line of reasoning may also be applicable to media violence. There is evidence that violent video games result in increased physiological arousal. Therefore, after playing them, our bodies need to rest—to return to baseline. This feeling tired or "spent" may be misinterpreted to suggest that we would act less aggressively, when in fact all it means is that our bodies are tired of the stress we have put on them from playing a violent game that increases heart rate, blood pressure, and stress hormone levels.

Public Policy

General Issues

The high exposure rates to media violence in general and the ever-increasing amount of exposure to increasingly graphic violent video games invite questions about public policy. Although we agree that both the general media violence and the specific video game violence research literatures are sufficiently mature and clear to warrant public policy debates, we also believe that it is important to keep our personal views on political solutions private so that we can focus on the scientific merits of the research literature and on various proposed public policies related to media violence. In recent years, we have learned that many well-meaning people do not understand that scientifically derived information does not and can not *automatically* translate into appropriate and effective public policy. This lesson has been driven home in our teaching undergraduate and graduate courses; through public lectures, seminars, and discussions with industry, legislative, First Amendment, and child advocacy groups; and in occasionally contentious debates with other behavioral scientists. Although we are not public policy experts, we believe that Figure 9.1 nicely illustrates at least four very different and important sources of information underlying the formulation of effective public policy: scientific, legal, personal values, and political realities.

Three of the four sources are sufficiently obvious that only brief explication is necessary. First, consider the role of relevant scientific theory and data, denoted by the label "Science Facts." Science facts refer to the relevant knowledge base, consisting of relevant theory created, revised, and supported by a diverse set of empirical studies generated by research scientists with an appropriate specialty. Such science facts can and should influence public policy in at least two major ways. First, well-developed science can identify societal problems that might benefit from some sort of public policy attention and intervention. For example, theory, empirical research, and the resultant scientific fact that tobacco smoking increases the likelihood of eventually contracting lung cancer served as an impetus to public policy debates and action, as well as to personal decisions regarding smoking even before any public policy changes were implemented. Simi-

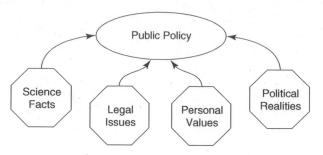

Figure 9.1 Relation of scientific information to public policy.

larly, theory, empirical research, and the resultant scientific fact that exposure to media violence increases the likelihood of aggressive behavior in
both short- and longer-term contexts has served as an impetus to recent
public policy debates and (we hope) to personal decisions by some people
to reduce their own or their children's exposure to this risk factor.

Second, well-developed science facts can identify policies that are
likely to work as well as those unlikely to work. For example, public education campaigns, warning labels, and stricter enforcement of legal restrictions on tobacco products have reduced smoking rates. Similarly, the Head
Start program (based in part on solid social science research) has proven to
be an effective public policy intervention, whereas non-research–based
programs (e.g., midnight basketball programs; scared straight) tend not to
fare very well. In both cases, identification of potential problems and identification of potentially fruitful public policies, science contributes by providing key answers to factual questions.

A second component of good public policy decision making concerns
legal issues. Of course, these issues vary greatly from one public policy
domain to another. One major legal issue in the media violence domain
concerns U.S. Constitution First Amendment questions about the legality
of government-imposed restrictions on access and exposure to violent materials by children and young adolescents (e.g., under the age of 21 or 18).
We are not legal scholars, and therefore do not pretend to have the answer
to the government restrictions question. However, we should point out that
there are government restrictions on children's access to pornography,
even though the research literature on the potential harmful effects of exposure to pornography is less massive and less conclusive than the literature on harmful media violence effects. Also, some leading First Amendment scholars have written persuasive accounts of how certain forms of
government restrictions on children's access to violent media would pass
all legal tests (e.g., Saunders, 2003a, 2003b).

A third component concerns political realities. What is likely to be popular with voters? Who has the money and clout to influence legislators? 'Nuff said.

The roles of the prior three components as sources of public policy input are fairly obvious. However, the fourth component, *personal values* as a source of legitimate input to public policy decisions, seems less clear. An example concerning strict versus loose handgun control laws may help. Any individual citizen, voter, legislator, civil servant, or other player in a public policy decision may have multiple personal values that are relevant to the decision. Assume for the moment that research on the effects of strict handgun laws conclusively demonstrates that such laws effectively reduce homicide rates.[1] Further assume that all legal issues have been resolved and that the political situation is such that such laws could be enacted and enforced. Does this mean that any rational individual must support such laws? We believe the answer is "no." Implicit in many gun control debates is the assumption that everyone agrees that lower homicide rates is a highly prized state of affairs—it is an important personal value for most people. And that probably is a correct assumption, although there are certainly individual differences in degree of importance attached to this personal value. But there are other important personal values that may, for some individuals, override the value they place on a lower homicide rate. Many U.S. citizens clearly value very highly the ability to purchase, own, and use handguns with little or no government interference. Some may hold this value to be more important than lower homicide rates. For them, it would be entirely rational to oppose a public policy of adding restrictions to handgun ownership and to vote for their local, state, and federal representatives with this issue factored into their voting decision. A similar rationale could apply in the media violence cases. In sum, scientific facts do not, cannot, and should not be the *sole* determinants of public policy, as illustrated in Figure 9.1.

Policy Debates and Industry Response

Returning to the media violence issue, note that both the general media violence research literature and the more specific video game violence research literature make it clear that one contributing cause of the continuing problems of aggression and violence in modern society is high levels of exposure to media violence that begin at ever-earlier ages. That is, the sci-

---

[1] Some would argue that such conclusive evidence already exists, whereas others would deny it. We make no claims about the gun control research literature, and merely ask the reader to assume, for the sake of the example, that there is clear, conclusive evidence.

ence facts in this domain are sufficiently clear to warrant public policy debates. In fact, a host of possible public policy actions have been debated for years, although few have been enacted, especially in the United States (unless one counts industry constructed and controlled rating systems). A brief history of some of the public policy debates on violent video games is presented below.

In 1993, U.S. Senators Joseph Lieberman and Herbert Kohl noticed the increasing violence in video games and held hearings to examine the issue. Although there was much less research on the effects of violent video games (partly because there was much less violence in video games in the 1980s), the senators put pressure on the video game industry to create a rating system. The goal of a rating system would be to provide information to parents about the content of games so that they could make informed decisions about which games their children could play. In response to this pressure the Entertainment Software Ratings Board was created in 1994 to begin rating games. In 1996, the Senators asked the National Institute on Media and the Family to conduct an annual *Video and Computer Game Report Card* (VGRC) to document how well the video game industry was following through on its commitments (report cards available at http://www.mediafamily.org/research/vgrc_index.shtml). The report card initially documented how well the rating system was being implemented, but as the industry changed and more research became available it broadened to cover several areas. In 1998 and 1999, the report card began to report how the video game industry appeared to be targeting young players (under 17) with advertisements for Mature (M) rated games, and how very few rental or retail stores enforced the ratings.

After the tragedy at Columbine High School in 1999, the country began questioning whether marketing violence to children was part of the problem. President Clinton asked the Federal Trade Commission to examine the marketing practices of the media industries, and discovered that 70% of M-rated games targeted children under 17 as their audience (FTC, 2000). Furthermore, they found that unaccompanied children aged 13 to 16 could purchase M-rated games 83% of the time. In response to these studies, the video game industry took a positive step in creating its Advertising Review Council to set policies and monitor the advertising, packaging, and promotional materials for video games (see http://www.esrb.org/arc.asp for more information). This responsible industry response made a significant improvement in advertising materials and placement.

In March, 2000, the U.S. Senate Committee on Commerce, Science, and Transportation held a hearing, "The Impact of Interactive Violence on Children," at which several researchers and several public policy advocates testified about the current state of research and problems being created by easy access to violent games (see http://www.psychology.iastate.edu/faculty/caa/abstracts/2000-2004/00Senate.html for some of the testimony). The industry refused to send a representative.

Research has continued to be conducted on several issues relevant to public policy, including the accuracy of the ratings and the effects of violent games. With regard to research on the validity of the ratings, Walsh & Gentile (2001) conducted a validity test of several rating systems that revealed there is less validity with the ratings than should be expected. In response to this study, the U.S. Senate again held hearings in 2001. Ultimately, the video game industry again acted responsibly to make some revisions to its rating system to help address some of the concerns. Additional research is necessary to determine whether the revisions were sufficient, though recent evidence (Haninger & Thompson, 2004) suggests major problems remain (for a review of issues surrounding media rating systems, see Gentile, Humphrey, & Walsh, 2005).

With regard to the effects of violent games, the video game industry does not appear to be responding in a responsible manner. The industry continues to give, at best, a mixed message to parents. On the one hand, they tout how good their rating system is (e.g., Entertainment Software Association, 2004), while simultaneously claiming (in television, newspaper, and magazine reports and interviews, in courtroom briefs, in conference addresses) that there is *no research* demonstrating that violent games can lead to negative outcomes. For example, Doug Lowenstein, president of the Entertainment Software Association, stated in a May 12, 2000 interview on CNN, "There is absolutely no evidence, none, that playing a violent video game leads to aggressive behavior." This clearly was not accurate at that time, and of course the research literature linking violent video games to aggressive behavior has gotten stronger since then. Nonetheless, Mr. Lowenstein continues to misinform the general public. In a PBS interview that aired at least twice in 2005 (summer and fall) he said, "Every independent researcher, meaning every researcher who has come to this without a preconceived notion trying to prove that video games are harmful has looked at the literature and said there is absolutely no evidence to suggest that violent video games are harmful." This statement and others like it are not only inaccurate, but they serve to confuse the public about why they should learn about and use the ratings, and almost certainly contribute to the lax attitudes and behavior exhibited by many parents.

One professional organization that does not doubt the serious aggression-teaching abilities is the United States Department of Defense. The U.S. Army recognized the benefits of video games for teaching skills, and licensed the popular violent video game series *Rainbow Six* to train their special operations forces because it is so good at teaching all of the steps necessary to plan and conduct a successful special ops mission (Ubi Soft, 2001). Furthermore, the Army has created its own video games. Some of these have been created initially by the Army to train its own forces, and then versions of them were repackaged and sold to the public. For example, the Army created a realistic military simulation game to train its soldiers in field tactics in a wide range of environments, which was then adapted and sold as *Full Spectrum Warrior* on the Xbox and PC platforms in 2003. More recently, the Marine Corps created a game titled *First to Fight* that is sold as a video game and is used as a Marine training tool. It is described as "a tactical first-person shooter in which you lead a four-man fire team in close-quarters urban combat in the streets and buildings of Beirut. It was created with the help of more than 40 active-duty U.S. Marines fresh from firefights in the Middle East and will be used by the United States Marine Corps for training" (www.firsttofight.com). Finally, the Department of Defense also uses video games as a recruiting tool. It created the video game *America's Army*, which is available for free download to anyone (www.americasarmy.com). In their own words, the game "is part of the Army's communications strategy. . . . The Army's game is an entertaining way for young adults to explore the Army and its adventures and opportunities as a virtual Soldier. As such, it is part of the Army's communications strategy designed to leverage the power of the Internet as a portal through which young adults can get a first hand look at what it is like to be a Soldier. The game introduces players to different Army schools, Army training, and life in the Army. Given the popularity of computer games and the ability of the Internet to deliver great content, a game was the perfect venue for highlighting different aspects of the Army" (America's Army, 2005). From the perspective of the armed services, the fact that video games can interest youth in violence, train them in tactics, and potentially disinhibit aggressive behaviors is a positive effect. From a general societal standpoint, however, it is unlikely that we desire children to grow up to be more aggressive and more effective in their aggression attempts.

In recent years the research on the negative effects of violent video games on children has become clearer and stronger, but recent attempts by the industry and various educational groups in the United States to reduce children's exposure to the most graphically violent games have yielded little improvement, as revealed by several recent studies of children's access to such games. Furthermore, several states and municipalities have passed legislation designed to provide information to parents and to restrict the sale or rental of the most violent games to children without parental consent. Unfortunately, instead of aiding in such attempts, the video game industry has actively worked against the passage of any such laws, going so far as to warn those involved in the legislative process that the industry will exact a huge price on them if the law under consideration is passed. And this has not been an idle threat. In the recent case concerning the law passed by the State of Illinois, for example, the Entertainment Software Association filed a petition in the U.S. District Court asking the court to order the State to pay them $644,545 in legal fees (Gamasutra, 2006). Furthermore, the industry has repeatedly gone to court to block enforcement of such laws, and so far has succeeded in all attempts. In addition, the media industry continues to deny the body of relevant research and to cast aspersions on those scientists who conduct research that finds evidence of harm. For example, in response to California Bill 1793, which would require stores to display signs and brochures explaining the video game ratings to customers, the president of the Interactive Entertainment Merchants' Association stated, "To date there has been no conclusive research to prove a causal linkage between playing videogames and asocial behavior" (Halpin, 2004). To support their claims, they often cite critics of media violence research, critics who typically have never conducted any original empirical scientific studies on violent video games and have sometimes been paid by the media industries to write critiques or to testify in court (see Huesmann & Taylor, 2003). Other critics from media industry simply invent stories about legitimate researchers that simply are untrue. For example, in his commentary on a 2003 conference in Australia on video games and rating systems, Julian Wood of the Australian online magazine *Filmink* wrote that, "Prof. Craig Anderson . . . received large sums of money to analyse other media violence studies," implying that prior reviews were biased in some way (Filmink, 2006). Not only is the statement untrue (none of us have ever received large sums of money to do a literature review), but it reveals that the author does not really understand scientific methods or ethics, or the advantages of meta-analyses used to summarize a body of research.

Another response by the industry and their supporters has been to state that researchers who find negative effects of violent video games already have their minds made up about the results of studies before they are conducted. The implication is that such researchers who find and report negative effects are not to be trusted, that somehow they are biasing or fabricating their data. Of course, this is not how science is conducted, and the fact that multiple research teams around the world are finding very similar effects, and that the research is being screened for quality and published in top peer-reviewed journals, demonstrates the validity and integrity of the existing research literature. Speaking personally, all of our studies (including those described in this volume) are designed to be able to show positive effects (e.g., lower aggression after violent video game play) as well as negative effects. Indeed, we would definitely prefer to discover that violent video games have no deleterious effects on children and adolescents. We could then turn our attention to other research matters (e.g., positive uses of video game technology) and avoid the vilification and other stresses and hassles inherent in defending the science. Unfortunately, that is not what the studies show, and we believe that the research (showing both positive and negative effects) is a valid part of public policy debates. In the following paragraphs we briefly describe several potential types of policies that should be considered. We do so, however, without endorsing any specific one, except perhaps the first one on education.

Policy Options

Education

One obvious solution is to provide much better public education about the deleterious effects of exposing children and youth to media violence. The main idea is that if people truly understood the consequences, they would cut consumption of violent media. There have been few efforts along this line, none in the United States, at least not with a major public (e.g., federal) funding component designed to guarantee that all parents and soon-to-be parents receive such education. There are numerous parent and child advocacy groups worldwide attempting to provide such education. The media violence consumption data demonstrate that such small, underfunded, piecemeal efforts have largely failed to influence the population in general. Whether a much larger educational effort comparable in scope to educational efforts concerning the effects of smoking on lung cancer would have a substantial effect is an open question.

Voluntary Ratings by the Industries

This has been the dominant approach in the United States for many years, although the "voluntary" label is not quite accurate. The ratings systems for television, films, music, and video games were in each case created only after Congress threatened the industries with government regulation. This ratings approach has obviously failed. There are several likely reasons for this. First, existing rating systems are flawed in numerous ways. They are based on invalid assumptions about what is safe versus harmful for different aged individuals, the rating criteria are frequently misapplied, the rating criteria have shifted (becoming more lenient) over time, and age-based systems often encourage underage consumption (Gentile et al., 2005). Second, the entertainment industries frequently fail to follow their own guidelines, thereby allowing (and in many cases actively encouraging) underage consumption. Third, many parents fail to understand the different rating systems or how to use them (does anybody know how to use the V-Chip?) and do not believe that there is any real need to screen their children from violent media.

Warning Labels

By warning labels, we do not mean the relatively uninformative kind presently used in the United States on music, which merely informs potential purchasers that some of the songs contain explicit lyrics. We mean labels much like those used on tobacco products that warn users of the negative effects of using the product. For instance, video games of the type that have been shown to produce negative effects could carry a warning like the following, "Warning: This video game contains violence. Playing violent video games increases the likelihood of aggressive behavior in the immediate situation. Repeatedly playing violent video games increases the likelihood of aggressive behavior across longer periods of time." Obviously, there are several important issues in the warning label approach, including the specific wording, whether it is mandatory or voluntary, and who decides which games (or films, television shows) should carry the warning label.

Licensing Requirements

Both radio and television broadcast frequencies are government controlled, based on the idea that the airwaves are a public good. "Owning" a broadcast license for a particular frequency in a particular region has always had at least some minimal requirement that some portion of the programming be devoted to the public good, usually in the form of educational programming. The Federal Communication Commission is the primary agency in the U.S. involved in regulating these industries. Over the years the FCC has pressured commercial radio and TV companies to provide better, more child- and family-friendly programming, with some limited success. However, many (e.g., DeGaetano, 2004; Grossman & DeGaetano, 1999; Steyer, 2002) believe that those limited successes have practically all disappeared in recent years, the result of major abrogation of responsibility by the FCC (and the industries it supposedly oversees) and of major technological changes in electronic media (e.g., cable television, digital television, computers, the Internet).

Mandatory Ratings by the Industries

Governments could require the industries to provide and enforce their own ratings systems. This has never been done in the United States or anywhere else as far as we know. In the United States the 1996 Telecommunications Act required that television ratings be created, but it did not specify how or by whom. We suspect that there would be many unsolvable problems with a government mandated, industry-controlled system.

Governmental Ratings of an Advisory Nature

Governments could create their own ratings systems and agencies, and require that all entertainment media products be rated by the government agency prior to distribution and sale. Many countries have such systems in place (e.g., Australia, United Kingdom). We know of no studies of their effectiveness in reducing children's exposure to harmful materials.

Mandatory Universal Ratings Provided or Validated by an Independent Third Party

Because multiple ratings systems are confusing and often contradictory for parents, governments could enact legislation requiring that the TV, film, music, and video game industries create one universal rating system so that parents need not learn the full "alphabet soup" of different ratings systems. Furthermore, legislation could mandate that the ratings be administered independently of each medium. (Currently, American TV ratings are assigned by the TV networks, film ratings are created by the Motion Picture Association of America, and so on.) Legislation might also mandate that an independent ratings review board be created to conduct research on the validity of the ratings and to maintain standards. Many industry representatives have argued that a universal ratings system is not possible, and that ratings systems must be different because the various media are different (e.g., Baldwin, 2001; Lowenstein, 2001; Rosen, 2001). These claims are unconvincing for at least three reasons. First, organizations like the National Institute on Media and the Family have already created universal ratings systems and applied them successfully across media types (e.g., Walsh, Gentile, & van Brederode, 2002). Second, although TV, films, music, and video games certainly are different in important ways, the concerns that parents have about violence, offensive language, and sexual content are similar across all types of media. Third, there has been some good research on how to create better and more effective ratings systems. It appears that such a system could be created and that there are several good options for selecting a third-party group to oversee the system.

Legal Access Restrictions

Governments could (and sometimes do) restrict access to certain types of material. Government-enforced age-based ratings and restrictions are fairly common in modern industrialized societies but are absent in the United States. Nonetheless, this approach seems feasible even in the *United States* for two reasons. First, the media industries already acknowledge that some media products are not appropriate for children (and give them R [film], TV-MA [TV], or M [video games] ratings). Second, legal precedent in the United States has established that the government has an entirely appropriate role in limiting the influences and activities to which children are exposed. For example, state and local authorities routinely restrict minors' access to tobacco, guns, pornography, and gambling. In fact, the U.S. Supreme Court, in *Ginsberg v. New York* (1968) upheld limiting minors' access to pornography on the basis of whether it was "rational for the legislature to find that the minors' exposure to [such] material *might be harmful*" (emphasis added). The research conducted to date has clearly met this test, demonstrating that exposing children and youth to violent media is harmful. With regard to video games, we find it odd that the video game industry has fought every legislative attempt to restrict the sale of M-rated games to minors. This is puzzling because it suggests that the industry is unwilling to stand behind its own ratings.

Governmental Restrictions on Production

Many governments (including the U.S. government) have made the production of certain types of materials illegal. For example, making sexually explicit films using minors is illegal in the United States. "Snuff" films, in which people are filmed being killed, are also illegal. In a sense, such productions are illegal because the activities involved in the making of such materials are themselves illegal (sex with a minor, murder). However, further restrictions on production of entertainment materials involving otherwise legal behaviors are likely to have the greatest problems, given the high value most people (ourselves included) place on freedom of expression.

10

Reducing Violent Video Game Effects

So how can the individual parent reduce the negative effects of exposure to violent video games, or to other forms of violent media? The careful reader may have noticed that most of the public policy options mentioned in the preceding section are directed primarily at reducing exposure of children and adolescents to such harmful materials. Of course, the most obvious way to reduce the harmful effects on children of any substance is to reduce or eliminate exposure to that substance, be it a drug (cocaine), a tool (sharp kitchen knife), or other product (lead-based paint, media violence). At this time, the best advice we can give concerning violent video games is also the most obvious—reduce as much as possible children's and adolescents' exposure to such violent games.

There is some limited evidence that explicit discussions with children and adolescents about the harmful effects of media violence and the inappropriateness of aggressive and violent solutions to interpersonal conflicts, and practice at thinking about potential nonviolent solutions to conflict, all guided by parents or other adult authority figures, might reduce the harmful effects of exposure to media violence (Huesmann, Eron, Klein, Brice, & Fischer, 1983; Robinson et al., 2001). Indeed, results we reported earlier from Studies 1 and 3 also suggest that adult involvement in children's media use might provide some protection against the harmful effects of violent video games. However, parents who merely play violent video games with their children are likely to make matters worse, rather than better. Such coplay without explicit discussions of harmful effects, inappropriateness of violent solutions in real life, and promotion of nonviolent alternatives is likely to be seen by the child as endorsement of violent attitudes and behaviors. Although there is no directly relevant video game research on this potential coplay effect, there is some research from the television domain (e.g., Nathanson, 1999).

In many of our presentations and conversations with parents and other caregivers, we are asked for guidelines and advice concerning video game use by children and adolescents. Table 10.1 contains some of our thoughts on this issue that we think will prove useful.

Providing clear science-based information to parents and caregivers about the harmful effects of exposure to violent video games is the first step in helping educate the people who are best able to use the information. This is why we believe that the video game industry should stop providing a mixed message to parents. Currently they praise their ratings system while simultaneously (and disingenuously) stating that there is no evidence that video games might have any harmful effects. Instead, they could use their powerful position to state that the reason parents *should* use the video game ratings and monitor what their children play is because the research demonstrates that video game play can and does have effects, both positive (e.g., of educational games) and negative (e.g., of violent games).

Concluding Thoughts

To date, there has been little serious public policy debate concerning how best to reduce exposure of children and youth to media violence. Many of the debates that have occurred—in Congress, the popular press, and conferences—have often focused on whether there is sufficient scientific evidence of harmful effects to even bother with considering public policy actions. Other debates have confused the basic scientific question of *whether* there are significant harmful effects with other public policy issues. For example, in the United States some of the most vociferous critics of media violence research are First Amendment proponents who do not seem to understand that the scientific question (are there harmful effects?) is different from the legal question (are proposed policies legal under the U.S. Constitution?).

As the medical, public health, and psychological scientific communities have repeatedly stated in recent years, the scientific debate about whether there are harmful effects of media violence is over. The present three studies further demonstrate such harmful effects in the video game domain, as well as provide additional confirmation of the bio-social-cognitive theoretical models (e.g., the General Aggression Model) used to understand human aggression. We believe that it is time for modern society to move

HELPFUL ADVICE FOR PARENTS AND OTHER CAREGIVERS ON CHOOSING AND USING VIDEO GAMES

Don't Rely Solely on Ratings

Even video games rated "E" for "Everyone" often contain a lot of violent action. Our own analysis of the Electronic Software Regulation Board's 2001 Web site database revealed that 87% of games rated "T" for "Teen" contained violence. The video game industry even markets their most violent games (rated "M" for "Mature" audiences at least 17 years old) to children, even those as young as six (Federal Trade Commission, 2000). Furthermore, anyone with an Internet connection can download violent video games for free and without proof of age. Indeed, a number of violent games can be played for free on the Internet.

How Can You Tell if a Video Game Is Potentially Harmful?

- Play the game, or have someone else demonstrate it for you.
- Ask yourself the following 6 questions:
  - Does the game involve some characters trying to harm others?
  - Does this happen frequently, more than once or twice in 30 minutes?
  - Is the harm rewarded in any way?
  - Is the harm portrayed as humorous?
  - Are nonviolent solutions absent or less "fun" than the violent ones?
  - Are realistic consequences of violence absent from the game?
- If two or more answers are "yes," think very carefully about the lessons being taught before allowing your child access to the game.

Be a Wise Consumer

- Buy video games that are helpful to your children
- Don't buy potentially harmful video games

Be a Wise Parent/Grandparent/Caregiver

- Know what your children are playing
- Don't allow access to violent video games
- Restrict time spent playing video games
- Explain to your children why violent games are harmful
- Teach nonviolent problem solving at every opportunity

Be an Involved Citizen/Consumer

- If a retailer sells violent games to children, complain to the owner or manager
- If a retailer screens sales or rental of violent materials to children, thank the owner or manager, perhaps by purchasing nonviolent educational video games
- Help educate others in your community (parents, youth, public officials)

(*continued*)

162

- Let your public officials know that you are concerned

Some Web Sites About Entertainment Media and Parenting Issues

- http://www.mediawise.org
- http://www.sosparents.org
- http://www.youngmedia.org.au/
- http://www.childrennow.org/
- http://www.kff.org/entmedia
- http://www.familymediaguide.com
- http://www.cmch.tv
- http://www.acmecoalition.org/
- http://www.vicparenting.com.au/vp/index.php

Our Web Sites, Which Provide Relevant Information, Interviews, and Publications

- http://www.psychology.iastate.edu/faculty/caa/index.html
- http://www.psychology.iastate.edu/faculty/dgentile/

on to the more difficult public policy questions concerning whether modern societies should take action to reduce the high rates of exposure of children and youth to media violence, and if so, what public policies would be likely to be the most effective. We also believe that the various constituencies within the video game industry (e.g., Entertainment Software Association, ESRB) could do themselves and modern society a lot of good by joining with relevant leading professional health associations, child advocacy groups, and the real scientific experts on media violence effects, child and adolescent development, and ratings systems to help create a voluntary educational and parental control system that truly works. We invite them to do so, and we would be happy to work with them on this important task.

Appendix 1: Best Practices Coding

The following potential methodological problems were examined for each sample:

1. Nonviolent video game condition contained violence, and there was no suitable nonviolent control condition.
2. Violent video game condition contained little or no violence.
3. Evidence that the violent and nonviolent conditions differed significantly in ways that could contaminate the conditions, such as the nonviolent condition being more difficult, boring, or frustrating than the violent condition.
4. A pre–post design was used, but only the average of the pre- and postmanipulation measures was reported.
5. Each research session involved both a video game player and an observer, but only the average of the player-observer measures was reported.
6. The aggressive behavior measure was not aggression against another person (e.g., aggression against a nonhuman character, or against objects).
7. The outcome variable was physiological arousal, but arousal differences between the violent and nonviolent video game conditions were already controlled by pretesting or game selection (i.e., equally arousing violent and nonviolent games were intentionally chosen by

Adapted from Anderson et al. (2004) with permission from Elsevier, Inc.

the researchers to control for potential arousal effects on other outcome measures such as aggressive behavior).

8. The outcome variable was aggressive affect, but affective differences between the violent and nonviolent video game conditions were already controlled by pretesting or game selection (i.e., violent and nonviolent games were intentionally chosen by the researchers to have the same affective impact, to control for potential affective influences on other outcome measures such as aggressive behavior).

9. In a correlational study, the measure of video game exposure was not specifically tied to violent video games (e.g., the amount of time spent on any kind of video game was measured instead of time spent on violent video games).

Some of these "weaknesses" are actually strengths for other aspects of the same research. For example, if one wants to study whether violent video game content (relative to a nonviolent video game) can increase aggressive behavior even when there are no arousal differences between the games, pretesting and selecting violent and nonviolent video games that produce equivalent levels of arousal is an excellent methodological feature. However, that same sample does not allow a good test of whether violent video games on average increase arousal. Thus, for aggressive behavior this sample could be coded as a "best practice" one, whereas it would be coded as a "not best practice" sample for physiological arousal.

Appendix 2: Video Game Ratings

Industry-based ratings are provided by the Entertainment Software Rating Board. Their Web site address is: www.esrb.org. The rating system has changed a number of times in recent years. Four of the games used in Study 1 of this monograph were from an earlier version of the rating system. The ratings and content descriptors for Study 1 games are shown in Table A1.

TABLE A1   Ratings and content descriptors for Study 1 games

Game Title/Platform Used*	Rating	Content Descriptors
Oh No! More Lemmings Macintosh*, Windows	E—Everyone	None

Captain Bumper
  Macintosh*
	No ESRB rating,
	  advertised as for
	  ages 8 and older
		Most people would consider
		  this to be a family-friendly
		  game

Otto Matic Macintosh*, Windows	E—Everyone	Violence
Street Fighter II Turbo PlayStation*, Windows	T—Teen	Animated violence

Future Cop L.A.P.D.
  Macintosh*, Windows,
  PlayStation, PS One
	T—Teen	Animated blood
		  Animated violence

Parents should keep in mind that scientific research has found instances of games that some parents and adolescents believe should have received stricter ratings than given by the ESRB (e.g., Funk et al., 1999; Walsh & Gentile, 2001) and games that contain potentially objectionable content that is not included in the official content descriptors (e.g., Haninger & Thompson, 2004; Thompson & Haninger, 2001; Thompson, Tepichin, & Haninger, 2006). Whether this is the result of ambiguous definitions, lack of reliability by the ESRB in applying their criteria, differences in criteria and definitions used by the ESRB raters and the raters in the scientific studies, or incomplete information being provided by the game publishers is unclear. It is likely that there are multiple sources of these discrepancies. Interestingly, there appears to be fairly high agreement at the extremes (games that have no violence whatsoever, and games that are extremely violent in content and graphicness). The majority of discrepancies appears to be with cartoonish violence, which is present in many E-Rated games. Nonetheless, such discrepancies occur for Teen- and Mature-rated games as well.

The ESRB ratings are based on videotapes supplied by the publisher, who is legally bound to capture all pertinent content, including the most extreme instances, across all relevant categories including but not limited to violence, language, sex, controlled substances and gambling. Game publishers must also submit a detailed written questionnaire to the ESRB, often with supplements (lyric sheets, scripts, etc.) specifying exactly what pertinent content will be in the game. The current official definitions of the ESRB rating system (http://www.esrb.org/ratings/ratings_guide.jsp) are as follows.

ESRB Game Ratings and Content Descriptors

The Entertainment Software Rating Board (ESRB) ratings are designed to provide information about video and computer game content, so you can make informed purchase decisions. ESRB ratings have two parts: *rating symbols* suggest age appropriateness for the game, and *content descriptors* indicate elements in a game that may have triggered a particular rating and/or may be of interest or concern.

To take full advantage of the ESRB rating system, it's important to check both the *rating symbol* (on the front of the game box) and the *content descriptors* (on the back of the game box)

Titles rated *EC (Early Childhood)* have content that may be suitable for ages three and older. Contains no material that parents would find inappropriate.

Titles rated *E (Everyone)* have content that may be suitable for ages six and older. Titles in this category may contain minimal cartoon, fantasy, or mild violence and/or infrequent use of mild language.

Titles rated *E10+ (Everyone 10 and older)* have content that may be suitable for ages 10 and older. Titles in this category may contain more cartoon, fantasy, or mild violence, mild language, and/or minimal suggestive themes.

Titles rated *T (Teen)* have content that may be suitable for ages 13 and older. Titles in this category may contain violence, suggestive themes, crude humor, minimal blood, simulated gambling, and/or infrequent use of strong language.

Titles rated *M (Mature)* have content that may be suitable for persons ages 17 and older. Titles in this category may contain intense violence, blood and gore, sexual content, and/or strong language.

Titles rated *AO (Adults Only)* have content that should only be played by persons 18 years and older. Titles in this category may include prolonged scenes of intense violence and/or graphic sexual content and nudity.

 Titles listed as *RP (Rating Pending)* have been submitted to the ESRB and are awaiting final rating. (This symbol appears only in advertising prior to a game's release.)

ESRB Content Descriptors

- *Alcohol Reference*—Reference to and/or images of alcoholic beverages
- *Animated Blood*—Discolored and/or unrealistic depictions of blood
- *Blood*—Depictions of blood
- *Blood and Gore*—Depictions of blood or the mutilation of body parts
- *Cartoon Violence*—Violent actions involving cartoon-like situations and characters. May include violence where a character is unharmed after the action has been inflicted
- *Comic Mischief*—Depictions or dialogue involving slapstick or suggestive humor
- *Crude Humor*—Depictions or dialogue involving vulgar antics, including "bathroom" humor
- *Drug Reference*—Reference to and/or images of illegal drugs
- *Edutainment*—Content of product provides user with specific skills development or reinforcement learning within an entertainment setting. Skill development is an integral part of product
- *Fantasy Violence*—Violent actions of a fantasy nature, involving human or non-human characters in situations easily distinguishable from real life
- *Informational*—Overall content of product contains data, facts, resource information, reference materials or instructional text
- *Intense Violence*—Graphic and realistic-looking depictions of physical conflict. May involve extreme and/or realistic blood, gore, weapons, and depictions of human injury and death
- *Language*—Mild to moderate use of profanity
- *Lyrics*—Mild references to profanity, sexuality, violence, alcohol, or drug use in music
- *Mature Humor*—Depictions or dialogue involving "adult" humor, including sexual references
- *Mild Violence*—Mild scenes depicting characters in unsafe and/or violent situations
- *Nudity*—Graphic or prolonged depictions of nudity
- *Partial Nudity*—Brief and/or mild depictions of nudity

- *Real Gambling*—Player can gamble, including betting or wagering real cash or currency
- *Sexual Themes*—Mild to moderate sexual references and/or depictions. May include partial nudity
- *Sexual Violence*—Depictions of rape or other violent sexual acts
- *Simulated Gambling*—Player can gamble without betting or wagering real cash or currency
- *Some Adult Assistance May Be Needed*—Intended for very young ages
- *Strong Language*—Explicit and/or frequent use of profanity
- *Strong Lyrics*—Explicit and/or frequent references to profanity, sex, violence, alcohol, or drug use in music
- *Strong Sexual Content*—Graphic references to and/or depictions of sexual behavior, possibly including nudity
- *Suggestive Themes*—Mild provocative references or materials
- *Tobacco Reference*—Reference to and/or images of tobacco products
- *Use of Alcohol*—The consumption of alcoholic beverages
- *Use of Drugs*—The consumption or use of illegal drugs
- *Use of Tobacco*—The consumption of tobacco products
- *Violence*—Scenes involving aggressive conflict

Online Rating Notice

Online games that include user-generated content (e.g., chat, maps, skins) carry the notice *Game Experience May Change During Online Play* to warn consumers that content created by players of the game has not been rated by the ESRB.

References

Abelson, R. P. (1985). A variance explanation paradox: When a little is a lot. *Psychological Bulletin, 97*, 129–133.

Aber, J. L., & Jones, S. J. (1997). Indicators of positive development in early childhood: Improving concepts and measures. In R. M. Hauser, B. V. Brown, & W. R. Prosser (Eds.), *Indicators of children's well-being* (pp. 395–408). New York: Sage Foundation.

America's Army Web site. (2005, October 12). FAQS. Accessed: March 23, 2006, from http://www.thearmygame.com/support/faq_win.php?p=1

Anderson, C.A. (1983). Motivational and performance deficits in interpersonal settings: The effect of attributional style. *Journal of Personality and Social Psychology, 45*, 1136–1147.

Anderson, C. A. (2003). Video games and aggressive behavior. In D. Ravitch and J. P. Vitcritti (Eds.), *Kid stuff: Marketing sex and violence to America's children* (pp. 143–167). Baltimore, MD: Johns Hopkins University Press.

Anderson, C. A. (2004). An update on the effects of violent video games. *Journal of Adolescence, 27*, 133–122.

Anderson, C. A., & Anderson, K. B. (1996). Violent crime rate studies in philosophical context: A destructive testing approach to heat and southern culture of violence effects. *Journal of Personality and Social Psychology, 70*, 740–756.

Anderson, C. A., Anderson, K. B., Dorr, N., DeNeve, K. M., & Flanagan, M. (2000). Temperature and aggression. *Advances in Experimental Social Psychology, 32*, 63–133.

Anderson, C. A., Benjamin, A. J., & Bartholow, B. D. (1998). Does the gun pull the trigger? Automatic priming effects of weapon pictures and weapon names. *Psychological Science, 9*, 308–314.

Anderson, C. A., Benjamin, A. J., Wood, P. K., & Bonacci, A. M. (2006). Development and testing of the Velicer Attitudes Toward Violence Scale: Evidence for a four-factor model. *Aggressive Behavior, 32*, 122–136.

Anderson, C. A., Berkowitz, L., Donnerstein, E., Huesmann, R. L., Johnson, J., Linz, D., Malamuth, N., & Wartella, E. (2003). The influence of media violence on youth. *Psychological Science in the Public Interest, 4*, 81–110.

Anderson, C. A., & Bushman, B. J. (1997). External validity of "trivial" experiments: The case of laboratory aggression. *Review of General Psychology, 1*, 19–41.

Anderson, C. A., & Bushman, B. J. (2001). Effects of violent video games on aggressive behavior, aggressive cognition, aggressive affect, physiological arousal, and prosocial behavior: A meta-analytic review of the scientific literature. *Psychological Science, 12,* 353–359.

Anderson, C. A., & Bushman, B. J. (2002a). Human aggression. *Annual Review of Psychology, 53,* 27–51.

Anderson, C. A., & Bushman, B. J. (2002b). The effects of media violence on society. *Science, 295,* 2377–2378.

Anderson, C. A., & Bushman, B. J. (2002c). Media violence and the American public revisited. *American Psychologist, 57,* 448–450.

Anderson, C. A., Bushman, B. J., & Groom, R. W. (1997). Hot years and serious and deadly assault: Empirical tests of the heat hypothesis. *Journal of Personality and Social Psychology, 73,* 1213–1223.

Anderson, C. A., & Carnagey, N. L. (2004). Violent evil and the general aggression model. Chapter in A. Miller (Ed.), *The social psychology of good and evil* (pp. 168–192). New York: Guilford Publications.

Anderson, C. A., Carnagey, N. L., Flanagan, M., Benjamin, A. J., Eubanks, J., & Valentine, J. C. (2004). Violent video games: Specific effects of violent content on aggressive thoughts and behavior. *Advances in Experimental Social Psychology, 36,* 199–249.

Anderson, C. A., & Dill, K. E. (2000). Video games and aggressive thoughts, feelings, and behavior in the laboratory and in life. *Journal of Personality & Social Psychology, 78,* 772–791.

Anderson, C. A., & Huesmann, L. R. (2003). Human aggression: A social-cognitive view. In M. A. Hogg & J. Cooper (Eds.), *Handbook of social psychology* (pp. 296–323). London: Sage Publications.

Anderson, C. A., Krull, D. S., & Weiner, B. (1996). Explanations: Processes and consequences. In E. T. Higgins & A. W. Kruglanski (Eds.), *Social psychology: Handbook of basic principles* (pp. 271–296). New York: Guilford Press.

Anderson, C. A., Lindsay, J. J., & Bushman, B. J. (1999). Research in the psychological laboratory: Truth or triviality? *Current Directions in Psychological Science, 8,* 3–9.

Anderson, C. A., & Murphy, C. R. (2003). Violent video games and aggressive behavior in young women. *Aggressive Behavior, 29,* 423–429.

Anderson, D. R., Huston, A. C., Schmitt, K. L., Linebarger, D. L., & Wright, J. C. (2001). Early childhood television viewing and adolescent behavior: The recontact study. *Monographs of the Society for Research in Child Development, 66* (1, Serial No. 264).

Anderson, K. B., Anderson, C. A., Dill, K. E., & Deuser, W. E. (1998). The interactive relations between trait hostility, pain, and aggressive thoughts. *Aggressive Behavior, 24,* 161–171.

Anthony, E. J. (1974). The syndrome of the psychologically invulnerable child. In E. Anthony & C. Koupernick (Eds.), *The child in his family: Vol 3. Children at psychiatric risk* (pp. 529–544). New York: John Wiley & Sons.

Aristotle. (1941). *Poetics.* In R. McKeon (Ed.) *The basic works of Aristotle.* New York: Random House.

Austin, E. W. (1993). Exploring the effects of active parental mediation of television content. *Journal of Broadcasting & Electronic Media, 37,* 147–158.

Baldwin, W. (2001). Testimony submitted to the Committee on Governmental Affairs, United States Senate. Accessed July 25, 2001, from http://www.senate.gov/~gov _affairs/072501_baldwin.htm

Banaji, M. R., & Crowder, R. G. (1989). The bankruptcy of everyday memory. *American Psychologist, 44*, 1185–1193.

Bandura, A. (1971). Psychotherapy based upon modeling principles. In A. E. Bergin and S. L. Garfield (Eds.), *Handbook of psychotherapy and behavior change*. New York: Wiley.

Bandura, A. (1973). *Aggression: A social learning theory analysis*. Englewood Cliffs, N.J.: Prentice-Hall.

Bandura, A. (1986). Social foundations of thought and action: A social cognitive theory. Englewood Cliffs, N.J.: Prentice-Hall.

Bandura, A., Ross, D., & Ross, S. A. (1961). Transmission of aggression through imitation of aggressive models. *Journal of Abnormal & Social Psychology, 63*, 575–582.

Bandura, A., Ross, D., & Ross, S. A. (1963). Imitation of aggression through imitation of film-mediated aggressive models. *Journal of Abnormal and Social Psychology, 66*, 3–11.

Baron, R. A., & Richardson, D. R. (1994). Human aggression, 2nd ed. New York: Plenum Press.

Bartholow, B. D., & Anderson, C. A. (2002). Examining the effects of violent video games on aggressive behavior: Potential sex differences. *Journal of Experimental Social Psychology, 38*, 283–290.

Bartholow, B. D., Anderson, C. A., Carnagey, N. L., & Benjamin, A. J. (2005). Interactive effects of life experience and situational cues on aggression: The weapons priming effect in hunters and nonhunters. *Journal of Experimental Social Psychology, 41*, 48–60.

Belsky, J., & Fearon, R.M.P. (2002). Infant-mother attachment security, contextual risk, and early development: A moderational analysis. *Development and Psychopathology, 14*, 293–310.

Belson, W. A. (1978). *Television violence and the adolescent boy*. Hampshire, England: Saxon House, Teakfield.

Berkowitz, L. (1984). Some effects of thoughts on anti- and prosocial influences of media events: A cognitive-neoassociation analysis. *Psychological Bulletin, 95*(3), 410–427.

Berkowitz, L. (1990). On the formation and regulation of anger and aggression: A cognitive-neoassociationistic analysis. *American Psychologist, 45*(4), 494–503.

Berkowitz, L. (1993). Aggression: Its causes, consequences, and control. New York: McGraw-Hill.

Berkowitz, L., & Donnerstein, E. (1982). External validity is more than skin deep: Some answers to criticism of laboratory experiments. *American Psychologist, 37*, 245–257.

Bernstein, S., Richardson, D., & Hammock, G. (1987). Convergent and discriminant validity of the Taylor and Buss measures of physical aggression. *Aggressive Behavior, 13*, 15–24.

Berry, J. W., Worthington, E. L., O'Connor, L. E., Parrott, L. III, Wade, N. G. (2005). Forgivingness, vengeful rumination, and affective traits. *Journal of Personality, 73*, 183–225.

Bjorkqvist, K. (1985). *Violent films, anxiety, and aggression*. Helsinki: Finnish Society of Sciences and Letters.

Bjorkqvist, K., Lagerspetz, K., & Kaukiainen, A. (1992). Do girls manipulate and boys fight? Developmental trends in regard to direct and indirect aggression. *Aggressive Behavior, 18*, 117–127.

Bonacci, A. M., Tapscott, R. L., Carnagey, N. L., Wade, N. G., & Gentile, D. A. (2004, May). The relationship between violent and relationally aggressive media consumption and interpersonal relations. Poster presented at the American Psychological Society 16th Annual Convention, Chicago, Ill.

Boyatzis, J., Matillo, G. M., & Nesbitt, K. M. (1995). Effects of the *Mighty Morphin Power Rangers* on children's aggression with peers. *Child Study Journal, 25*, 45–55.

Buchanan, A. M., Gentile, D. A., Nelson, D., Walsh, D. A., & Hensel, J. (2002, August). *What goes in must come out: Children's media violence consumption at home and aggressive behaviors at school.* Paper presented at the International Society for the Study of Behavioural Development Conference, Ottawa, Ontario, Canada.

Buchman, D. D., & Funk, J. B. (1996). Video and computer games in the '90s: Children's time commitment and game preference. *Children Today, 24*, 12–16.

Bushman, B. J. (1995). Moderating role of trait aggressiveness in the effects of violent media on aggression. *Journal of Personality and Social Psychology*, 69, 950–960.

Bushman, B. J. (2002). Does venting anger feed or extinguish the flame? Catharsis, rumination, distraction, anger, and aggressive responding. *Personality & Social Psychology Bulletin, 28*, 724–731.

Bushman, B. J., & Anderson, C. A. (1998). Methodology in the study of aggression: Integrating experimental and nonexperimental findings. In R. Geen and E. Donnerstein (Eds.), *Human aggression: Theories, research, and implications for policy.* (pp. 23–48). San Diego: Academic Press.

Bushman, B. J., & Anderson, C. A. (2001). Is it time to pull the plug on the hostile versus instrumental aggression dichotomy? *Psychological Review, 108*, 273–279.

Bushman, B. J., & Anderson, C. A. (2002). Violent video games and hostile expectations: A test of the general aggression model. *Personality and Social Psychology Bulletin, 28*, 1679–1686.

Bushman, B. J., Baumeister, R. F., & Stack, A. D. (1999). Catharsis, aggression, and persuasive influence: Self-fulfilling or self-defeating prophecies? *Journal of Personality and Social Psychology, 76*, 367–376.

Bushman, B. J., & Huesmann, L. R. (2001). Effects of televised violence on aggression. In D. Singer & J. Singer (Eds.), *Handbook of children and the media* (pp. 223–254). Thousand Oaks, Calif.: Sage Publications.

Buss, A. H., & Perry, M. (1992). The aggression questionnaire. *Journal of Personality and Social Psychology*, 63, 452–459.

Campbell, A. (1993). *Men, women and aggression.* New York: Basic Books.

Carlson, M., Marcus-Newhall, A., & Miller, N. (1989). Evidence for a general construct of aggression. *Personality and Social Psychology Bulletin, 15*, 377–389.

Carnagey, N. L., & Anderson, C. A. (2003). Theory in the study of media violence: The general aggression model. In D. A. Gentile, (Ed.), *Media violence and children,* (pp. 87-106). Westport, Conn.: Praeger.

Carnagey, N. L., & Anderson, C.A. (2005). The effects of reward and punishment in violent video games on aggressive affect, cognition, and behavior. *Psychological Science, 16*, 882–889.

Carnagey, N. L., & Anderson, C. A., Bushman, B. J. (in press). The effect of video game violence on physiological desensitization to real-life violence. *Journal of Experimental Social Psychology.*

Cicchetti, D., & Toth, S. L. (1998). The development of depression in children and adolescents. *American Psychologist, 53,* 221–241.

CIRP. (1998, 2005). *Cooperative Institutional Research Program survey results.* Ames, Iowa: Office of Institutional Research.

Cohen, J. (1988). *Statistical power analysis for the behavioral sciences* (2nd ed.) Hillsdale, N.J.: Lawrence Erlbaum Associates.

Comstock, G. (1980). New emphases in research on the effects of television and film violence. In E. L. Palmer & A. Dorr (Eds.), *Children and the faces of television: Teaching, violence, selling* (pp. 129–148). New York: Academic Press.

Comstock, G., & Scharrer, E. (2003). Meta-analyzing the controversy over television violence and aggression. In D. A. Gentile (Ed.), *Media violence and children* (pp. 205-226). Westport, Conn.: Praeger.

Copycat Crimes, Issue Brief Series. (2000). Studio City, Calif.: Mediascope Press. Retrieved Sept 13, 2004, from http://www.mediascope.org/pubs/ibriefs/cc.htm

Crick, N. R. (1995). Relational aggression: The role of intent attributions, feelings of distress, and provocation type. *Development and Psychopathology, 7,* 313–322.

Crick, N. R. (1996). The role of overt aggression, relational aggression, and prosocial behavior in children's future social adjustment. *Child Development, 67,* 2317–2327.

Crick, N. R., & Dodge, K. A. (1994). A review and reformulation of social information-processing mechanisms in children's social adjustment. *Psychological Bulletin, 115,* 74–101.

Crick, N. R., & Dodge, K. A. (1996). Social information-processing mechanisms in reactive and proactive aggression. *Child Development, 67,* 993–1002.

Crick, N., & Grotpeter, J. (1995). Relational aggression, gender, and social-psychological adjustment. *Child Development, 66,* 710–722.

Crick, N. R., Werner, N. E., Casas, J. F., O'Brien, K. M., Nelson, D.A., Grotpeter, J. K., & Markon, K. (1999). Childhood aggression and gender: A new look at an old problem. In D. Bernstein (Ed.), *Nebraska symposium on motivation: Gender and motivation, 45,* 75–141. Lincoln, Neb.: University of Nebraska Press.

DeGaetano, G. (2004). *Parenting well in a media age: Keeping our kids human.* Fawnskin, Calif.: Personhood Press.

Dill, K. E., Anderson, C. A., Anderson, K. B., & Deuser, W. E. (1997). Effects of aggressive personality on social expectations and social perceptions. *Journal of Research in Personality,* 31, 272–292.

Dill, K. E., & Dill, J. C. (1998). Video game violence: A review of the empirical literature. *Aggression and Violent Behavior: A Review Journal, 3,* 407–428.

Dodge, K. A, & Crick, N. R. (1990). Social information-processing bases of aggressive behavior in children. *Personality and Social Psychology Bulletin, 16,* 8–22.

Dodge, K. A., & Petit, G. S. (2003). A biopsychosocial model of the development of chronic conduct problems in adolescence. *Developmental Psychology, 39,* 349–371.

Dominick, J. R. (1984). Videogames, television violence, and aggression in teenagers. *Journal of Communication, 34,* 136–147.

Donnerstein, E., & Berkowitz, L. (1981). Victim reactions in aggressive erotic films as a factor in violence against women. *Journal of Personality and Social Psychology, 41,* 710–724.

Donnerstein, E., Slaby, R. G., & Eron, L. D. (1994). The mass media and youth aggression. In L. D. Eron, J. H. Gentry, & P. Schlegel (Eds.), *Reason to hope: A psychoso-*

cial perspective on violence and youth (pp. 219–250). Washington, DC: American Psychological Association.

Dorr, A., & Rabin, B. E. (1995). Parents, children, and television. In M. Bornstein (Ed.), *Handbook of parenting: Vol. 4* (pp. 323–351). Mahwah, NJ: Erlbaum.

Durkin, K., & Barber, B. (2002). Not so doomed: Computer game play and positive adolescent development. *Applied Developmental Psychology, 23,* 373–392.

Economist. (2005, August 4). Breeding evil? *The Economist.* Downloaded March 23, 2006, from http://www.economist.com/printedition/displaystory.cfm?Story_ID= 4247084

Elliot, D. S., Huizinga, D., & Ageton, S. S. (1985). *Explaining delinquency and drug use.* Beverly Hills: Sage.

Entertainment Software Association. (2004). *Games, parents and ratings.* Available from http://www.theesa.com/pressroom.html

Eron, L. D., Huesmann, L. R., Lefkowitz, M. M., & Walder, L. O. (1972). Does television violence cause aggression? *American Psychologist, 27,* 253–263.

Federal Trade Commission. (2000). Marketing violent entertainment to children: A review of self-regulation and industry practices in the motion picture, music recording, and electronic game industries. Retrieved December 22, 2003, from http://www.ftc.gov/reports/index.htm#2000

Filmink. (2006). *Monkey see, monkey don't.* Downloaded on March 29, 2006, from www.filmink.com.au/search/displayarticle.asp?article_id=2172

Fiore, M. C., Smith, S. S., Jorenby, D. E., & Baker, T. B. (1994). The effectiveness of the nicotine patch for smoking cessation. *Journal of the American Medical Association, 271,* 1940–1947.

Fitzgerald, P., & Asher, S. R. (1987, August). Aggressive-rejected children's attributional biases about liked and disliked peers. Paper presented at the annual meeting of the American Psychological Association, New York.

Funk, J. B. (1993). Reevaluating the impact of video games. *Clinical Pediatrics, 32,* 86–90.

Funk, J. B., Baldacci, H. B., Pasold, T., & Baumgardner, J. (2004). Violence exposure in real-life, video games, television, movies, and the Internet: Is there desensitization? *Journal of Adolescence, 27,* 23–39.

Funk, J. B., Flores, G., Buchman, D. D., & Germann, J. N. (1999). Rating electronic games: Violence is in the eye of the beholder. *Youth & Society, 30,* 283–312.

Gamasutra. (2006). *ESA Files to Retrieve Illinois Game Bill Legal Costs.* Downloaded on March 29, 2006 from www.gamasutra.com/php-bin/news_index.php?story=8544

Geen, R. G. (1990). *Human aggression.* Pacific Grove, Calif.: McGraw Hill.

Geen, R. G. (2001). *Human aggression.* Philadelphia, Penn.: Open University Press.

Geen, R. G., & O'Neal, E. C. (1969). Activation of cue-elicited aggression by general arousal. *Journal of Personality and Social Psychology, 11,* 289–292.

Geen, R. G., & Quanty, M. B. (1977). The catharsis of aggression: An evaluation of a hypothesis. In L. Berkowitz (ed.), *Advances in Experimental Social Psychology, 10,* 1–37.

Geen, R. G., & Thomas, S. L. (1986). The immediate effects of media violence on behavior. *Journal of Social Issues, 42(3),* 7–27.

Gentile, D. A. (Ed.) (2003). *Media violence and children.* Westport, Conn.: Praeger.

Gentile, D. A., & Anderson, C. A. (2003). Violent video games: the newest media violence hazard. In D. Gentile (ed.), *Media violence and children* (pp. 131–152). Westport, Conn.: Praeger.

Gentile, D. A. & Gentile, J. R. (under review). *Video games as exemplary teachers: A conceptual analysis.*

Gentile, D. A., Humphrey, J., & Walsh, D. A. (2005). Media ratings for movies, music, video games, and television: A review of the research and recommendations for improvements. *Adolescent Medicine Clinics, 16,* 427–446.

Gentile, D. A., Linder, J. R., & Walsh, D. A. (2003, April). *Looking through time: A longitudinal study of children's media violence consumption at home and aggressive behaviors at school.* Paper presented at the 2003 Society for Research in Child Development Biennial Conference, Tampa, Fla.

Gentile, D. A., Lynch, P. L., Linder, J. R., & Walsh, D. A. (2004). The effects of violent video game habits on adolescent hostility, aggressive behaviors, and school performance. *Journal of Adolescence, 27,* 5–22.

Gentile, D. A., & Sesma, A. (2003). Developmental approaches to understanding media effects on individuals. In D. A. Gentile, (Ed.), *Media violence and children* (pp. 19–38). Westport, Conn.: Praeger.

Gentile, D. A., & Walsh, D. A. (2002). A normative study of family media habits. *Journal of Applied Developmental Psychology, 23,* 157–178.

Gerbner, G., Gross, L., Morgan, M., & Signorielli, N. (1982). Charting the mainstreaming: Television's contributions to political orientations. *Journal of Communication, 32,* 100–127.

Giancola, P. R. (2003). The moderating effects of dispositional empathy on alcohol-related aggression in men and women. *Journal of Abnormal Psychology, 112,* 275–281.

Giancola, P. R., & Chermack, S. T. (1998). Construct validity of laboratory aggression paradigms: A response to Tedeschi and Quigley (1996). *Aggression and Violent Behavior, 3,* 237–253.

Ginsberg v. New York, 390 U. S. 629 (1968).

Glantz, M.D., & Johnson, J. L. (Eds.) (1999). *Resilience and development: Positive life adaptations.* New York: Kluwer.

Graybill, D., Kirsch, J. R., & Esselman, E. D. (1985). Effects of playing violent versus nonviolent video games on the aggressive ideation of aggressive and nonaggressive children. *Child Study Journal, 15,* 199–205.

Grossman, D., & DeGaetano, G. (1999). Stop teaching our kids to kill: A call to action against Tv, movie, and video game violence. Crown Publishers.

Halpin, H. (2004, September 24). IEMA criticizes Governor Schwartzenegger. [Press Release.] Available: http://www.gameindustry.com/ih/item.asp?id=330

Haninger, K., & Thompson, K. M. (2004). Content and ratings of teen-rated video games. *Journal of the American Medical Association, 291,* 856–65.

Harris, M. B., & Williams, R. (1985). Video games and school performance. *Education, 105*(3), 306–309.

Havighurst, R. J. (1949). *Developmental tasks and education.* Chicago: University of Chicago Press.

Hearold, S. (1986). A synthesis of 1043 effects of television on social behavior. In G. Comstock (Ed.), *Public communication and behavior* (Vol. 1, pp. 66-133). New York: Academic Press.

Hemphill, J. F. (2003). Interpreting the magnitudes of correlation coefficients. *American Psychologist, 58,* 78–79.

Huesmann, L. R. (1986). Psychological processes promoting the relation between exposure to media violence and aggressive behavior by the viewer. *Journal of Social Issues, 42*(3), 125–139.

Huesmann, L. R., & Eron, L. D. (Eds.). (1986). *Television and the aggressive child: A cross-national comparison.* Hillsdale, N.J.: Erlbaum.

Huesmann, L. R., Eron, L. D., Klein, R., Brice, P., & Fischer, P. (1983). Mitigating the imitation of aggressive behaviors by changing children's attitudes about media violence. *Journal of Personality and Social Psychology, 44,* 899–910.

Huesmann, L. R., & Miller, L. S. (1994). Long-term effects of repeated exposure to media violence in childhood. In L. R. Huesmann (Ed.), *Aggressive behavior: Current perspectives,* 153–186, New York: Plenum Press.

Huesmann, L. R., Moise, J. F., & Podolski, C. L. (1997). The effects of media violence on the development of antisocial behavior. In D. M. Stoff, J. Breiling, & J.D. Maser (Eds.), *Handbook of antisocial behavior* (pp. 181–193). New York: John Wiley & Sons.

Huesmann, L. R., Moise-Titus, J., Podolski, C. L., & Eron, L. D. (2003). Longitudinal relations between children's exposure to TV violence and their aggressive and violent behavior in young adulthood: 1977–1992. *Developmental Psychology, 39,* 201–221.

Huesmann, L. R., & Taylor, L. D. (2003). The case against the case against media violence. In D. A. Gentile (Ed.), *Media violence and children* (pp. 107-130). Westport, Conn.: Praeger.

Ihori, N., Sakamoto, A., Kobayashi, K., & Kimura, F. (2003). Does video game use grow children's aggressiveness?: Results from a panel study. In K. Arai (Ed.), *Social contributions and responsibilities of simulation and gaming* (pp. 221–230). Tokyo: Japan Association of Simulation and Gaming.

Irwin, A. R., & Gross, A. M. (1995). Cognitive tempo, violent video games, and aggressive behavior in young boys. *Journal of Family Violence, 10,* 337–350.

Janko, R. (1987). Introduction. *Aristotle's Poetics.* Indianapolis, Ind.: Hackett Publishing.

Johnson, J. G., Cohen, P., Smailes, E. M., Kasen, S., & Brook, J. S. (2002). Television viewing and aggressive behavior during adolescence and adulthood. *Science, 295,* 2468–2471.

Jordan, A. (2004). The role of media in children's development: An ecological perspective. *Developmental and Behavioral Pediatrics, 25,* 196–206

Keller, W. (2002, August 10). *Wrestling's state of business is taking more knocks then [sic] deserved.* Retrieved November 1, 2002, from http://www.pwtorch.com/artman/publish/printer_163.shtml

Kenny, D. A. (1984). The NBC study and television violence: A review. *Journal of Communication, 34,* 176–188.

Kent, S. L. (2001). *The ultimate history of video games.* Roseville, Calif.: Prima Publishing.

Kirsh, S. J. (1998). Seeing the world through "Mortal Kombat" colored glasses: Violent video games and the development of a short-term hostile attribution bias. *Childhood, 5,* 177–184.

Kirsh, S. J. (2003). The effects of violent video game play on adolescents: The overlooked influence of development. *Aggression and Violent Behavior: A Review Journal, 8,* 377–389.

Kirsh, S. J. (2006). Children, adolescents, and media violence: A critical look at the research. Thousand Oaks, Calif.: Sage Publications.

Kirsh, S. J., Olczak, P. V., & Mounts, R. W. (2005). Violent video games induce an affect processing bias. *Media Psychology, 7,* 239–250.

Krahé, B., & Möller, I. (2004). Playing violent electronic games, hostile attributional style, and aggression-related norms in German adolescents. *Journal of Adolescence, 27,* 53–69.

Kruglanski, A. W. (1975). The human subject in the psychology experiment: Fact and artifact. In L. Berkowitz (Ed.), *Advances in experimental social psychology, vol. 8* (pp. 101–147). New York: Academic Press.

Lagerspetz, K. M., & Bjorkqvist, K. (1992). Indirect aggression in girls and boys. In L. R. Huesmann (Ed.), *Aggressive behavior: Current perspectives* (pp. 131–50). New York: Plenum.

Lagerspetz, K. M., Bjorkqvist, K., & Peltonen, T. (1988). Is indirect aggression typical of females? Gender differences in aggressiveness in 11- to 12-year-old children. *Aggressive Behavior, 14,* 403–414.

Larson, R. (2001). Commentary: Children and adolescents in a changing media world. *Monographs of the Society for Research in Child Development, 66* (1, Serial No. 264).

Lefkowitz, M. M., Eron, L. D., Walder, L. O., & Huesmann, L. R. (1972). Television violence and child aggression: A follow-up study. In G. A. Comstock & E. A. Rubenstein (Eds.), *Television and social behavior.* Vol. 3: Washington, D.C.: U.S. Government Printing Office.

Lefkowitz, M. M., Eron, L. D., Walder, L. O., & Huesmann, L. R. (1977). *Growing up to be violent: A longitudinal study of the development of aggression.* New York: Pergamon Press.

Leyens, J. P., Camino, L., Parke, R. D., & Berkowitz, L. (1975). Effects of movie violence on aggression in a field setting as a function of group dominance and cohesion. *Journal of Personality and Social Psychology, 32,* 346–360.

Lin, C. A. & Atkin, D. J. (1989). Parental mediation and rulemaking for adolescent use of television and VCRs. *Journal of Broadcasting & Electronic Media, 33,* 53–67.

Linz, D., Donnerstein, E., & Adams, S. M. (1989). Physiological desensitization and judgments about female victims of violence. *Human Communication Research, 15,* 509–522.

Lowenstein, D. (2001). Testimony submitted to the Committee on Governmental Affairs, United States Senate. Accessed July 25, 2001, from http://www.senate.gov_affairs/072501_lowenstein.htm

Malamuth, N. M. & Impett, E. A. (2001). Research on sex in the media. In D. G. Singer & J. L. Singer (Eds.), *Handbook of children and the media* (pp. 269–287). Thousand Oaks, Calif.: Sage Publications.

Masten, A. S. (2001). Ordinary magic: Resilience processes in development. *American Psychologist, 56,* 227–238.

Masten, A. S., & Braswell, L. (1991). Developmental psychopathology: An integrative framework. In P. R. Martin (Ed.), *Handbook of behavior therapy and psychological science: An integrative approach* (pp. 35–56). New York: Pergamon Press.

Masten, A. S., & Coatsworth, J. D. (1998). The development of competence in favorable and unfavorable environments: Lessons from research on successful children. *American Psychologist, 53,* 205–220.

Masten, A. S., Hubbard, J. J., Gest, S. D., Tellegen, A., Garmezy, N., & Ramirez, M. (1999). Competence in the context of adversity: Pathways to resilience and maladaptation from childhood to late adolescence. *Development and Psychopathology, 11,* 143–169.

Masten, A. S., Miliotis, D., Graham-Bermann, S. A., Ramirez, M., & Neemann, J. (1993). Children in homeless families: Risks to mental health and development. *Journal of Consulting and Clinical Psychology, 61,* 335–343.

Masten, A. S., & Reed, M. G. J. (2002). Resilience in development. In S. R. Snyder & S. J. Lopez (Eds.), *The handbook of positive psychology* (pp. 74–88). New York: Oxford University Press.

Masten, A. S., & Wright, M. O. (1998). Cumulative risk and protective models of child maltreatment. In B. B. R. Rossman & M. S. Rosenberg (Eds.), *Multiple victimization of children: Conceptual, developmental, research, and treatment issues* (pp. 7–30). Binghamton, N.Y.: Haworth.

McCloskey, M. S., Berman, M. E., Noblett, K. L., & Coccaro, E. F. (2006). Intermittent explosive disorder-integrated research diagnostic criteria: Convergent and discriminant validity. *Journal of Psychiatric Research, 40,* 231–242.

McIntyre, J. J., & Teevan, J. J. Jr. (1972). Television violence and deviant behavior. In G. A. Comstock & E. A. Rubinstein (Eds.), *Television and Social Behavior: Television and Adolescent Aggressiveness: Vol. 3* (pp. 383–435). Washington, D.C.: U.S. Government Printing Office.

McLeod, J. M., Atkin, C. K., & Chaffee, S. H. (1972). Adolescents, parents, and television use: Adolescent self-report measures from Maryland and Wisconsin samples. In G. A. Comstock & E. A. Rubinstein (Eds.), *Television and Social Behavior: Television and Adolescent Aggressiveness: Vol. 3* (pp. 173–238). Washington, D.C.: U.S. Government Printing Office.

Milavsky, J. R., Kessler, R., Stipp, H., & Rubens, W. S. (1982). Television and aggression: Results of a panel study. In D. Pearl, L. Bouthilet, & J. Lazar (Eds.), *Television and behavior: Ten years of scientific progress and implications for the eighties: Vol. 2. Technical reviews* (DHHS Publication No. ADM 82-1196, pp. 138–157). Washington, D.C.: U.S. Government Printing Office.

Mischel, W. (1973). Toward a cognitive social learning reconceptualization of personality. *Psychological Review, 80,* 252–283.

Mischel, W., & Shoda, Y. (1995). A cognitive-affective system theory of personality: Reconceptualizing situations, dispositions, dynamics, and invariance in personality structure. *Psychological Review, 102,* 246–268.

Mook, D. G. (1983). In defense of external invalidity. *American Psychologist, 38,* 379–387.

Nathanson, A. I. (1999). Identifying and explaining the relationship between parental mediation and children's aggression. *Communication Research, 26,* 124–143.

National Commission on the Causes and Prevention of Violence. (1969). *Commission statement on violence in television entertainment programs.* Washington, D.C.: U.S. Government Printing Office.

National Institute of Mental Health. (1982). *Television and behavior: Ten years of scientific progress and implications for the eighties: Vol. 1. Summary report* (DHHS Publication No. ADM 82-1195). Washington, D.C.: U.S. Government Printing Office.

Needleman, H. L., & Gatsonis, C. A. (1990). Low-level lead exposure and the IQ of children. *Journal of the American Medical Association, 263,* 673–678.

Nelson, D. A., & Crick, N. R. (1999). Rose-colored glasses: Examining the social information-processing of prosocial young adolescents. *Journal of Early Adolescence, 19,* 17–38.

New York Times, (1964). Quote from *Correct Quotes, version 1.0.* WordStar International Incorporated, 1990.

Nisbett, R. E., & Cohen, D. (1996). *Culture of honor: The psychology of violence in the South.* Boulder, CO: Westview Press.

O'Donnell, C. R. (1995). Firearm deaths among children and youth. *American Psychologist, 50,* 771–776.

Office of Institutional Research. (1998, 2002). *Cooperative Institutional Research Program Survey Results.* Ames, Iowa: Author.

Ostrov, J. M., Gentile, D. A., & Crick, N. R. (in press). Media exposure, aggression and prosocial behavior during early childhood: A longitudinal study. *Social Development.*

O'Toole, M. E. (2000). *The school shooter: A threat assessment perspective.* Washington, D.C.: U.S. Department of Justice, Federal Bureau of Investigation.

Paik, H., & Comstock, G. (1994). The effects of television violence on antisocial behavior: A meta-analysis. *Communication Research, 21,* 516–546.

Parke, R.D., Berkowitz, L., Leyens, J.P., West, S. G., & Sebastian, R.J. (1977). Some effects of violent and nonviolent movies on the behavior of juvenile delinquents. In L. Berkowitz (Ed.), *Advances in Experimental Social Psychology, 10,* 135–172.

Petit, G. S. (2004). Violent children in developmental perspective: Risk and protective factors and the mechanisms through which they (may) operate. *Current Directions in Psychological Science, 13,* 194–197.

Petit, G. S., & Dodge, K. A. (2003). Violent children: Bridging development, intervention, and public policy. *Developmental Psychology, 39,* 187–188.

Potter, W. J. (1999). *On media violence.* Thousand Oaks, Calif.: Sage Publications.

Potter, W. J. (2003). *The 11 Myths of Media Violence.* Thousand Oaks, Calif.: Sage Publications.

Pratchett, R. (2005, December). *Gamers in the UK: Digital play, digital lifestyles.* London: BBC. Available: http://open.bbc.co.uk/newmediaresearch/2006/01/bbc_uk_games_research.html

Robinson, T. N., Wilde, M. L., Navracruz, L.C., Haydel, K. F., & Varady, A. (2001). Effects of reducing children's television and video game use on aggressive behavior: A randomized controlled trial. *Archives of Pediatric Adolescent Medicine, 155,* 17–23.

Rosen, H. (2001). Testimony submitted to the Committee on Governmental Affairs, United States Senate. Accessed July 25, 2001, from http://www.senate.gov/~gov_affairs/072501_rosen.htm

Rosenthal, R. (1986). Media violence, antisocial behavior, and the social consequences of small effects. *Journal of Social Issues, 42,* 141–154.

Rosenthal, R. (1990). How are we doing in soft psychology? *American Psychologist, 45,* 775–777.

Rutter, M. (2000). Resilience reconsidered: Conceptual considerations, empirical findings, and policy implications. In J. P. Shonkoff & S. J. Meisels (Eds.), *Handbook of Early Childhood Intervention* (2nd ed.) (pp. 651–682). Cambridge: Cambridge University Press.

Rutter, M. (2003). Commentary: Causal processes leading to antisocial behavior. *Developmental Psychology, 39,* 372–378.

Rutter, M., Maughan, B., Meyer, J., Pickles, A., Silberg, J., Simonoff, E., & Taylor, E. (1997). Heterogeneity of antisocial behavior: Causes, continuities, and consequences. *Nebraska Symposium on Motivation: Motivation and Delinquency, 44,* 45–118.

Sameroff, A. J., & Fiese, B. H. (2000). Transactional regulation: The developmental ecology of early intervention. In J. P. Shonkoff & S. J. Meisels (Eds.), *Handbook of early childhood intervention* (2nd ed.) (pp. 135–159). Cambridge: Cambridge University Press.

Sameroff, A. J., Seifer, R., & Bartko, W. T. (1997). Environmental perspectives on adaptation during childhood and adolescence. In S. S. Luthar, J. A. Burack, D. Ciccetti, & J. R. Weisz (Eds.), *Developmental psychopathology: Perspectives on adjustment, risk, and disorder* (pp. 507–526). New York: Cambridge Press.

Saunders, K. W. (2003a). Regulating youth access to violent video games: Three responses to First Amendment concerns. *2003 Michigan State Law Review, 51,* 51–114.

Saunders, K. W. (2003b). *Saving our children from the first amendment.* New York: New York University Press.

Schneider, W., & Shiffrin, R. M. (1977). Controlled and automatic human information processing: I. Detection, search, and attention. *Psychological Review, 84,* 1–66.

Sedikides, C., & Skowronski, J. J. (1990). Towards reconciling personality and social psychology: A construct accessibility approach. *Journal of Social Behavior and Personality, 5,* 531–546.

Sherry, J. L. (2001). The effects of violent video games on aggression: A meta-analysis. *Human Communication Research, 27,* 409–431.

Siegel, A. E. (1958). The influence of violence in the mass media upon children's role expectations. *Child Development, 29,* 35–56.

Slater, M. D., Henry, K. L., Swaim, R. C., Anderson, L. L. (2003). Violent media content and aggressiveness in adolescents: A downward spiral model. *Communication Research, 30,* 713–736.

Smith, A. H., Handley, M. A., & Wood, R. (1990). Epidemiological evidence indicates asbestos causes laryngeal cancer. *Journal of Occupational Medicine, 32,* 499–507.

Smith, S. L., & Donnerstein, E. (1998). Harmful effects of exposure to media violence: Learning of aggression, emotional desensitization, and fear. In R. Geen & E. Donnerstein, (Eds), *Human aggression: Theories, research, and implications for social policy* (pp. 167–202). San Diego, Calif.: Academic Press.

Sroufe, L. A. (1979). The coherence of individual development: Early care, attachment, and subsequent developmental issues. *American Psychologist, 34,* 834–841.

Sroufe, L. A. (1995). Emotional development: The organization of emotional life in the early years. New York: Cambridge Press.

Sroufe, L. A., Cooper, R. G., & DeHart, G. B. (1996). *Child development: Its nature and course* (3rd ed.). New York: McGraw-Hill.

Sroufe, L. A., Egeland, B., & Carlson, E. A. (1999). One social world: The integrated development of parent-child and peer relationships. In W. A. Collins & B. Laursen (Eds.), *Relationships as developmental context: The 30th Minnesota symposium on child psychology.* Hillsdale, N.J.: Erlbaum.

Steyer, J. P. (2002).*The other parent.* New York: Atria Books.

Strasburger, V. C., & Wilson, B. J. (2003). Television violence. In D. A. Gentile, (Ed.), *Media violence and children* (pp. 57–86). Westport, Conn.: Praeger.

Tamborini, R., Skalski, P., Lachlan, K., Westerman, D., Davis, J., & Smith, S. L. (2005). The raw nature of televised professional wrestling: Is the violence a cause for concern? *Journal of Broadcasting & Electronic Media, 49,* 202–220.

Taylor, M., & Flavell, J. H. (1984). Seeing and believing: Children's understanding of the distinction between appearance and reality. *Child Development, 55,* 1710–1720.

Thomas, M. H., Horton, R. W., Lippincott, E. C., & Drabman, R. S. (1977). Desensitization to portrayals of real life aggression as a function of television violence. *Journal of Personality and Social Psychology, 35,* 450–458.

Thompson, K. M., & Haninger, K. (2001). Violence in E-rated video games. *Journal of the American Medical Association, 286,* 591–598.

Thompson, K. M., Tepichin, K., & Haninger, K. (2006). Content and ratings of mature-rated video games. *Archives of Pediatric and Adolescent Medicine, 160,* 402–410.

Todorov, A., & Bargh, J. A. (2002). Automatic sources of aggression. *Aggression and Violent Behavior, 7,* 53–68.

Tukey, J. W. (1977). *Exploratory data analysis.* Menlo Park, Calif.: Addison-Wesley.

Ubi Soft. (2001). *Ubi Soft licenses Tom Clancy's Rainbow Six Rogue Spear game engine to train U.S. soldiers.* Accessed Feb 12, 2002, from http://corp.ubisoft.com/pr_release_010829a.htm.

Uhlmann, E., & Swanson, J. (2004). Exposure to violent video games increases automatic aggressiveness. *Journal of Adolescence, 27,* 41–52.

U.S. Department of Health and Human Services. (2001). *Youth violence: A report of the Surgeon General.* Rockville, MD: U.S. Department of Health and Human Services, Centers for Disease Control and Prevention, National Center for Injury Prevention and Control; Substance Abuse and Mental Health Services Administration, Center for Mental Health Services; and National Institutes of Health, National Institute of Mental Health.

U.S. Surgeon General's Scientific Advisory Committee on Television and Social Behavior. (1972). *Television and growing up: The impact of televised violence* (DHEW Publication No. HSM 72-9086). Washington, D.C.: U.S. Government Printing Office.

Walsh, D. (1999). *1999 Video and Computer Game Report Card.* Retrieved December 20, 1999, from http://www.mediaandthefamily.org/1999vgrc2.html

Walsh, D. (2000). *Fifth annual video and computer game report card.* Minneapolis, Minn.: National Institute on Media and the Family.

Walsh, D. A., & Gentile, D. A. (2001). A validity test of movie, television, and video-game ratings. *Pediatrics, 107,* 1302–1308.

Walsh, D., Gentile, D. A., Gieske, J., Walsh, M., & Chasco, E. (2003). *Eighth annual Mediawise video game report card.* Minneapolis: National Institute on Media and the Family.

Walsh, D. A., Gentile, D. A., & van Brederode, T. M. (2002). Parents rate the ratings: A test of the validity of the American movie, television, and video game ratings. *Minerva Pediatrica, 54,* 1–11.

Weigman, O., & van Schie, E.G.M. (1998). Video game playing and its relations with aggressive and prosocial behaviour. *British Journal of Social Psychology, 37,* 367–378.

Wells, A. J. (1998). Lung cancer from passive smoking at work. *American Journal of Public Health, 88,* 1025–1029.

Welten, D. C., Kemper, H.C.G., Post, G. B., & van Staveren, W. A. (1995). A meta-analysis of the effect of calcium intake on bone mass in young and middle aged females and males. *Journal of Nutrition, 125,* 2802–2813.

Williams, D., & Skoric, M. (2005). Internet fantasy violence: A test of aggression in an online game. *Communication Monographs, 72,* 217-233.

Wood, W., Wong, F. Y., & Chachere, J. G. (1991). Effects of media violence on viewers' aggression in unconstrained social interaction. *Psychological Bulletin, 109,* 371-383.

Woodard, E. H., & Gridina, N. (2000). *Media in the home.* Philadelphia, Penn.: Annenberg Public Policy Center of the University of Pennsylvania.

Woodward, G. C. & Denton, Jr., R. E. (2000). *Persuasion & influence in American life* (4th Ed.). Prospect Heights, Ill.: Waveland Press.

Zillmann, D. (1983). Arousal and aggression. In R. Geen & E. Donnerstein (Eds.), *Aggression: Theoretical and empirical reviews: Vol. 1* (pp. 75–102). New York: Academic Press.

Index